# Justice at the Margins

OTHER BOOKS BY KURT STRUCKMEYER:

*A Conspiracy of Love: Following Jesus in a Postmodern World* (2016, 2024)

*An Unorthodox Faith: A New Reformation for a Postmodern World* (2017)

*People of the Way: Passion and Resistance in a Postmodern World* (2023)

# Justice at the Margins

Jesus' Parables of Defiance and Disruption

## KURT STRUCKMEYER

RESOURCE *Publications* · Eugene, Oregon

JUSTICE AT THE MARGINS
Jesus' Parables of Defiance and Disruption

Resource Publications
An Imprint of Wipf and Stock Publishers
199 W. 8th Ave., Suite 3
Eugene, OR 97401

www.wipfandstock.com

PAPERBACK ISBN: 979-8-3852-3237-6
HARDCOVER ISBN: 979-8-3852-3238-3
EBOOK ISBN: 979-8-3852-3239-0

VERSION NUMBER 092624

To my grandchildren
Henry, Jasper, Wyatt, and Phoebe.

May you work toward a better world
where children no longer weep from poverty and hunger,
where they no longer live in fear from violence,
and where they are taught kindness, compassion, and love.

Love freely.
Act compassionately.
Live justly.
Seek peace.

# CONTENTS

# ABBREVIATIONS

| | |
|---|---|
| Dan | Daniel |
| Deut | Deuteronomy |
| ESV | English Standard Version |
| Eze | Ezekiel |
| Gal | Galatians |
| Gen | Genesis |
| Isa | Isaiah |
| Lev | Leviticus |
| Matt | Matthew |
| NET | New English Translation |
| NLT | New Living Translation |
| NRSV | New Revised Standard Version |
| Thom | Thomas |
| Tob | Tobit |

# INTRODUCTION

*The delusion of the oppressor is to expect a person
to ask nicely for the knife to be removed from their chest.
The demand for "civility" in the immediacy of violence
is a technique of distraction, not care.*

—COLE ARTHUR RILEY (B. 1990)

THIS BOOK CAME TO me unexpectedly, almost like a whirlwind. I had just released my third book, *People of the Way*, and was thinking it was probably my last, when I watched MSNBC's "The Last Word with Lawrence O'Donnell" on April 26, 2023. Guest host Ali Velshi (b. 1969) was filling in for Lawrence O'Donnell (b. 1951) and had a panel of three guests on: Zooey Zephyr, Maxwell Frost, and Justin Jones—all young legislators who had recently been in the news.

## ZOOEY ZEPHYR

Zooey Simone Zephyr (b. 1988) was 34 years old at the time of the interview and is a member of the Millennial generation. A bisexual trans woman, she was born in Billings, Montana as Zachary Raasch. She graduated from the University of Washington in Seattle in 2011 with a dual Bachelor of Arts in Business Administration and Creative Writing. Zephyr subsequently returned to her home state to pursue graduate studies at the University of Montana. She joined the university's Biology department and then the Office of the Provost, where she worked as a Program Manager overseeing the university's curricula. She worked to help university programs integrate diversity, equity, and inclusion practices into their faculty requirements, and worked with the city of Missoula, Montana to draft human rights legislation tailored towards making justice more accessible to people who have been discriminated against.

Zephyr became involved in activism in 2020. She testified before the Montana legislature in defense of LGBTQ+ rights and met with Republican Governor Greg Gianforte (b. 1961), but felt her words were not heard. Having watched bills limiting the rights of transgender people pass with one-vote margins, such as legislation making it difficult for transgender people to update birth certificates, she felt she needed to "get into the room where the laws are being written." Zephyr decided to run for state representative in the 2022 mid-term elections representing District 100 in Missoula. That November, Zephyr became the first openly trans woman to be elected to the Montana legislature alongside SJ Howell (b. 1980), the first nonbinary person to be elected. Zephyr assumed office in January 2023.

During a floor debate on April 18, 2023, Zephyr spoke passionately to convey just how dangerous and violent any legislation would be that sought to limit or eliminate the rights of transgender people to seek gender-affirming care in Montana. She admonished those who supported Senate Bill 99, which prohibits gender-affirming medical and surgical care for transgender minors. She first commented, "If you are forcing a trans child to go through puberty when they are trans, that is tantamount to torture, and this body should be ashamed." When this remark triggered an objection from the Republican majority leader, Zephyr replied, "The only thing I will say is if you vote 'yes' on this bill and 'yes' on these amendments, I hope the next time there's an invocation, when you bow your heads in prayer, you see the blood on your hands." This prompted a backlash from House Republicans who voted 68–32 along party lines to bar Zephyr from the House floor, gallery, and antechamber until the adjournment of the 2023 session the first week of May, effectively silencing her and the people she represented. She was permitted to vote remotely for the remainder of the session. Her crime? Zooey Zephyr was said to have breached the decorum of the House.

The bill was passed by the House and was signed into law by Governor Gianforte on April 28, 2023. It was also opposed by Mr. Gianforte's son, David Gianforte (b. 1991) who identifies as non-binary and had asked his father to reject what he called "immoral and unjust" bills backed by Republicans.

In 2023, the Human Rights Campaign (HRC), the nation's largest lesbian, gay, bisexual, transgender, and queer civil rights organization, was tracking more than 450 anti-LGBTQ+ bills that have been introduced in statehouses across the country.

## MAXWELL FROST

Maxwell Alejandro Frost (b. 1997) was just 26 years old at the time of the interview and is the youngest person and first member of Generation Z elected to the U.S. Congress. He represents the 10th congressional district in Orlando, Florida. Frost says he has worked as an advocate full-time since graduating from high school at Osceola County School for the Arts in Kissimmee, Florida because he couldn't afford to attend a typical 4-year university. He's currently enrolled at Valencia College in Orlando and says he plans on finishing his degree while serving in Congress.

Frost, who is black and Latino, has roots in a broad swath of American life. His parents, who adopted Frost at birth, are a Cuban American woman and a white man from Kansas. His birth parents were a Puerto Rican woman of Lebanese descent and a Haitian man. He spoke both English and Spanish at home, and he capitalized on his multicultural upbringing to campaign in a district that is as diverse as his own origins.

He first became involved in politics at age 16 after 20 children and six adults were fatally shot at Sandy Hook Elementary School in 2012. He became a volunteer lobbyist with the Newtown Action

Alliance, was an organizer with the American Civil Liberties Union, and eventually became the National Organization Director for March for Our Lives, the gun violence prevention group created in the wake of the 2018 school shooting in Parkland, Florida.

## JUSTIN JONES

Justin Shea Bautista-Jones (b. 1995) was just 27 years old at the time of the interview and is also a member of Generation Z. He is a Democratic member of the Tennessee House of Representatives for District 52, representing parts of Nashville.

Jones was born in Oakland, California to a Filipina mother and an African American father. He earned a Bachelor of Arts degree from Fisk University and is currently enrolled at Vanderbilt Divinity School in Nashville.

In 2019, he campaigned for the removal of a bust of Nathan Bedford Forrest (1821–1877)—a Confederate general during the Civil War and the first Grand Wizard of the Ku Klux Klan—from the Tennessee State Capitol. In July 2021, Tennessee officials voted to move Forrest's bust from the State Capitol to the Tennessee State Museum.

In the summer of 2020, Jones organized a 62-day sit-in protest for racial justice outside the state capitol after the murder of George Floyd (1973–2020). He was arrested and faced a total of 14 charges, including assault and reckless endangerment. All charges were eventually dismissed. He recounted the story of the event in *The People's Plaza: 62 Days of Nonviolent Resistance* (2022), with a foreword written by Yale professor and social activist Rev. William Barber II (b. 1963).

After the March 27, 2023, Covenant School shooting in Nashville that killed three nine-year-old children and three adult employees, Jones joined a March 30th protest by students, parents, and teachers for gun control reform, both outside and inside the state capitol along with house members Justin Pearson and Gloria Johnson. As the protesters filled House galleries, the three legislators approached the front of the House chamber with a bullhorn and participated in a chant, disrupting House proceedings. Republicans called the protest "disorderly behavior." The speaker of the House, Cameron Sexton (b. 1970), compared the three lawmakers to the rioters who breached the U.S. Capitol in 2021. He called their actions unacceptable and a violation of House rules of decorum and procedure. One Republican representative said the three Democrats had "effectively conducted a mutiny" and accused Jones of acting with disrespect and showing no remorse.

Jones, Pearson, and Johnson became known as "The Tennessee Three," and in a dramatic act of political retribution, the Republican-dominated Tennessee House voted on whether to expel the three members, which requires a two-thirds majority or 66 votes. Jones was expelled by a vote of 72–25; Pearson was expelled by a vote of 69–26; Johnson, who is a white 60-year-old representing District 90 of Knoxville, was spared her ouster by just one vote, 65–30. Republican legislators then passed resolutions that accused each of the three Democrats of engaging in "disorderly behavior" and purposely bringing "disorder and dishonor to the House of Representatives." In response Jones said, "We called for you all to ban assault weapons, and you respond with an assault on democracy."

Vice President Kamala Harris traveled to Nashville to meet with the three Tennessee Democrats a day after state Republican lawmakers ousted the two black members. During her remarks at Fisk University, Harris said the three Democrats were "channeling" the voices of their constituents during the protest. She continued, "A democracy says you don't silence the people. You do not stifle the people; you don't turn off their microphones when they are speaking about the importance of life and liberty."

On April 10, 2023, the Nashville Metropolitan Council voted unanimously to reinstate Jones to serve as an interim representative pending a special election to fill the seat. Then in August 2023, he defeated a Republican opponent with nearly 80 percent of the vote for the seat representing House District 52.

President Joe Biden was critical of the expulsions, calling them "shocking, undemocratic, and without precedent." He said,

"Rather than debating the merits of the issue of gun control, these Republican lawmakers have chosen to punish, silence, and expel duly-elected representatives of the people of Tennessee." Biden met with Justin Jones, Justin Pearson, and Gloria Johnson at the White House on Monday April 24, 2023.

In late August, during a special session to address public safety, Tennessee's House Republicans again silenced Justin Jones after he was deemed to have violated new stringent rules of decorum. Democrats stated that it was unclear exactly what Mr. Jones had said that was deemed off-topic, though Speaker of the House Cameron Sexton repeatedly maintained that a violation had occurred.

## JUSTIN PEARSON

The other Justin (b. 1995), also part of Generation Z, did not appear on MSNBC the night of the interview. He was born in Memphis, Tennessee. His father is a preacher who earned a Master of Divinity at Howard University in Washington DC, and his mother is a teacher. In 2017, Pearson graduated from Bowdoin College in Brunswick, Maine, majoring in Government and Legal Studies with a minor in Education Studies. He was elected in January 2023 to represent District 86, covering parts of the city of Memphis. While being sworn into the House, he wore a dashiki, a traditional West African garment, which complemented his Afro haircut. A Tennessee House Republican commented that dress norms for the House are a way to demonstrate respect, specifically mentioning that a tie was expected, and another Tennessee House Republican tweeted to Pearson, "Perhaps you should explore a different career opportunity." At ages 28 and 27, Pearson and Jones were the youngest members of the Tennessee House.

On April 12, six days after his expulsion, Pearson was reappointed to the Tennessee House following a unanimous vote by the Shelby County Board of Commissioners. In August 2023, Pearson defeated his Republican rival with more than 90 percent of the vote for the House District 86 seat.

## YOUNG AND FED UP

All of these young people represent constituents in largely "blue cities" in predominantly "red states." They are speaking on behalf of racial justice, gun reform, and LGBTQ+ rights in legislatures where they are largely disregarded by Republicans.

On April 26, 2023, Justin Jones joined a rally in Washington, DC with Maxwell Frost. "We're here today, to put it quite simply, because we're young and fed up," Frost said to supporters and press outside the Capitol. "Earlier this month, this nation watched in horror as innocent school children in Nashville were murdered in their classrooms." Then Jones addressed the crowd. "We come with a message from the Tennessee capitol to the U.S. Capitol: that we are fed up with the attacks on our democracy and we are fed up with the endless cycle of mass shootings. We are fed up with legislators and politicians who are trapped in the politics of racism. We are fed up, and when you are fed up, you've got to rise up."

## DISRUPTING ORDER

Maintaining decorum—behavior in keeping with good taste and propriety—is the dominant theme among Republican lawmakers who are seeking to control dissent. The status quo of racism, transphobia, and the killing of children and their teachers in their classrooms, hides behind a veneer of politeness, gentility, etiquette, and good manners. It becomes disrupted when people speak the truth.

Disrupting decorum, upsetting the social order, confronting racism, disturbing the status quo, and shameless behavior on behalf of justice are the themes I want to explore in this book. I recalled some work I had done back in 1998 on the parables of Jesus, studies for an adult Bible class I led at the time. The parables deal with the nature of the kingdom of God—ideas of holiness and sinfulness, of good people and bad, of purity and corruption. It seemed like a good time to review that work, present it to a larger audience, and see if it could shed any light on the present moment.

These are parables of resistance, disruption, and defiance for people living on the margins of society who are seeking dignity, equality, and justice.

# CHAPTER 1

# JESUS, THE STORYTELLER

*This is why I speak to them in parables,*
*because "they look but do not see*
*and hear but do not listen or understand."*[1]

—JESUS OF NAZARETH (c. 6 BCE–c. 30 CE)

*They strain their ears and never catch on;*
*For the hearts of these people are hard,*
*And their ears are dull,*
*And their eyes are dim.*
*Otherwise, their eyes might see,*
*And their ears might hear,*
*And their hearts might understand,*
*And they might turn around,*
*And I'll make them well.*[2]

—THE PROPHET ISAIAH
(8TH CENTURY BCE–7TH CENTURY BCE)

1. Matthew 13:13.
2. Isa 6:9–10. Translation by Jordan, *Cotton Patch Matthew and John*, 48.

Jesus was a teacher. During his lifetime his followers, opponents, and even interested inquirers regularly addressed him as "teacher." (Rabbi means "teacher.") One of the key tools of his teaching was storytelling. Jesus was a perfector of the form. Virtually nothing the authentic Jesus says is found in lecture form; instead, every word the synoptic gospels record is communicated through metaphor, parable, or simile. Through vivid parables of seeds, pearls, leaven, wayward children, rich men, poor widows, and day laborers, he helps us imagine the kingdom of God.

First-century Palestine was a culture based on oral communication. Over 95 percent of the people were illiterate, however Jesus' audience were steeped in stories. Much of the Hebrew Bible is a collection of the unique stories that shaped Israel as a people. Stories invite us in. As a type of picture language, stories help us see, even when we don't want to see. They help us understand, even when we have closed our minds.

The English word *parable* comes from the Greek word *parabolē* (*par-ab-ol-AY*), which means "to place alongside." So, a parable compares one thing to another. In the gospels, they are specifically used to compare some aspect of common, everyday life to some reality of the kingdom of God.

The parable is a well-conceived and artfully structured trap. It invites the listener into a simple story or comparison. It gets the listener comfortable with the familiar territory of the scene. Then the parable switches everything around and frustrates the expectations of the listener. For the listener, the parable is a story that comes out wrong. They are often shocking, scandalous, and startling. Or at least they were originally, before we domesticated them. And that started with the gospel writers, the first domesticators of the parables of Jesus.

Parables can shatter the deep structure of our accepted world. To hear a parable is to submit oneself to entering its world, to make oneself vulnerable. Parables have hooks all over them. They can grab each of us in a different way, according to our need.

The parables of Jesus were intended to show his listeners, both then and now, that the way the kingdom of God operates is not what we expect. The parables challenge comfortable beliefs and conventional wisdom about wealth and poverty, about holiness and sinfulness, about good people and bad, about purity and corruption, even about religion and beliefs. Theology teacher John Donahue (b. 1933) says that Jesus told parables that "took the side of the outcast, provoked the proud, and unsettled the complacent."[3]

## TAKING SIDES

I used to accept many of the conventional interpretations of the parables, that they were about miraculous growth or grace or prayer or humility. At least that is what the gospel writers said they were about. Some were interpreted as example stories—go and do likewise. Usually, they were interpreted as allegories with a rich man, a vineyard owner, or a judge as a stand-in for God. Then I read a book that changed my mind: *Parables as Subversive Speech: Jesus as Pedagogue of the Oppressed* by William R. Herzog II (1944–2019).

Herzog said,

> *The parables were not earthly stories with heavenly meanings but earthy stories with heavy meanings, weighted down by an awareness of the workings of exploitation in the world of their hearers. The focus of the parables was not on a vision of the glory of the kingdom of God, but on the gory details of how oppression served the interests of a ruling class. Instead of reiterating the promise of God's intervention in human affairs, they explored how human beings could respond to break the spiral of violence and cycle of poverty created by exploitation and oppression. The parable was a form of social analysis every bit as much as it was a form of theological reflection.*[4]

I believe that Herzog got much right in his analysis of a select group of parables, but at the same time his interpretations may have missed other aspects. I believe that some parables simply

---

3. Donahue, *Gospel in Parable*, 215.

4. Herzog, *Parables as Subversive Speech*, 3.

describe the kingdom of God as a prescriptive remedy for social injustice and as a way to stir the pot of a stifling status quo. But I credit Herzog with crafting creative alternatives and unexpected readings on a number of the parables.

Herzog stated that in their current narrative settings the parables serve the theological needs of the gospel writers. You can usually tell this is so if the gospel writer attempts to explain the parable, often putting the interpretation on the lips of Jesus. However, if they served the needs of Jesus' own teaching to his audience, and not of the gospel writers, they should be analyzed so as to make that distinction clear.

This is not a scholarly or academic work. There are many scholarly books about the parables of Jesus on the market, and I encourage you to read them. Instead, I shall take a layman's approach to presenting a select group of parables in a simple and easy manner. I shall show how the parables when separated from their gospel context can be interpreted differently and I shall attempt to analyze them in terms of their original first-century context. Hopefully, I shall present them in a way that preserves their original shock, scandal, defiance, and disturbance to their intended audience.

## THE JESUS SEMINAR

There are forty-three parables found in the gospels. Only twenty-four of them are deemed authentic (rated pink or red) by the Jesus Seminar. The remaining nineteen parables are deemed suspect (gray or black).

The Jesus Seminar was created almost 40 years ago, in 1985, to determine which words and actions can be reliably traced back to the historical Jesus. Made up of more than two hundred scholars, the seminar met twice a year to debate technical papers. At the end of presentations and debate, they then voted on whether the saying(s) attributed to Jesus could be deemed authentic or was more likely the creation of the early church. Dropping colored beads into a box determined whether a particular saying was red ("That's Jesus"), pink ("Sure sounds like Jesus"), gray ("Well, maybe"), or black ("There's been some mistake"). In 1993, the members of the Jesus Seminar published their findings in *The Five Gospels: the Search for the Authentic Words of Jesus*. The fifth gospel was the gospel of Thomas. The book includes a new translation from Greek texts (the Scholars Version) and an accompanying commentary explaining their conclusions. The twelve parables that follow are chosen from the twenty-four deemed pink (nineteen) and red (five).

## A NEW METAPHOR

At the heart of the gospel of Jesus is *the kingdom of God*. This one phrase sums up the entire ministry of Jesus and his whole life's work. As we read the gospels of Matthew, Mark, and Luke, we see that every thought and saying of Jesus was directed and subordinated to one single thing: the realization of the reign of God's love, compassion, and peace within human society. Jesus spoke of the kingdom of God more than any other subject.

Yet as a metaphor, *the kingdom of God* does not work very well for us today, nor will it conceivably work any better in the future. Kingdoms and empires are diminishing around the world. Democracies are rising, or in some cases, holding on precariously. But no matter what form governments take, structural domination systems abound. So, it would be helpful to find a new metaphor that people can better understand and connect with in the twenty-first century. We need a fresh language that will better describe the vision of Jesus and our role as his followers in a postmodern world. Brian McLaren (b. 1956) put it this way:

> When Jesus spoke of the kingdom of God, his language was charged with urgent political, religious, and cultural electricity. But today, if we speak of the kingdom of God, the original electricity is largely gone, and in its place, we often find a kind of tired familiarity that inspires not hope and excitement, but anxiety or boredom . . .

*For many people today, kingdom language evokes patriarchy, chauvinism, imperialism, domination, and a regime without freedom—the very opposite of the liberating, barrier-breaking, domination-shattering, reconciling movement the kingdom of God was intended to be! . . . If Jesus were here today, I'm quite certain he wouldn't use the language of kingdom at all, which leaves us wondering how he would articulate his message.*[5]

For some time, I have been using *"the conspiracy of love"* as a new metaphor for what Jesus was describing, especially considering his parables of the mustard seed and the leaven that have conspiratorial elements. I see the conspiracy of love as the subversive activity of a people focused on Jesus' vision of a better world—a world governed by love. The word *conspiracy* derives from the same root as *spirit*. The Latin root *spirare* (SPEE-rah-reh) means *to breathe*. For example, the word *respiration* is *to breathe again,* and *inspiration* means *to breathe in*—to be filled with the spirit. To *conspire* normally connotes agreement or unity in an activity, but it literally means *to breathe together*. Those engaged in a conspiracy are so united around an idea or action that they are seen to breathe as one. I believe that Jesus called his followers to engage in a conspiracy of profound personal and social transformation that would undermine the domination system in every time and place. It begins with acts of disruption and resistance, defiance and disobedience, rebelliousness and insubordination.

## GOD IS COMPASSIONATE LOVE

I also want to justify my substitution of the word "love" for "God." In my opinion, one does not have to believe in God—at least not in the traditional sense of a supernatural all-powerful being—to engage in the conspiracy of love.

Let me take a moment to describe what a non-supernatural, non-theistic God looks like. A remarkable document in the New Testament—the First Letter of John—introduced a

5. McLaren, *Everything Must Change*, 138–139.

completely different way of thinking about God than our traditional conception.

> *God is love, and he who abides in love abides in God, and God abides in him.*[6]

As far as I know, the New Testament has only three definitions for God: God is spirit,[7] God is light,[8] and God is love.[9] The first definition comes from the gospel of John and the second two derive from the First Letter of John. So, these metaphors may derive from the same community. But of all these definitions, love represents the highest, deepest, and most powerful force in human life. It is the energy that fosters human growth and change. Love is the impulse behind empathy and concern, and the fuel that drives compassion and justice.

In Greek, *God is love* is *theos ein agapē* (THEH-ohs ayn ag-AH-pay). *Agapē* (ag-AH-pay) is one of four different Greek words which we translate into English as love. *Philia* (fil-EE-ah) refers to loyal friendship or a brotherly love; *eros* (ERR-ohs) is used to describe passionate erotic or romantic love; and *storgē* (STOR-gay) is used in relation to the natural affection of family love, like the love of a parent for a child. But *agape* implies a *selfless love*, a *self-giving love*, often an *unconditional love*. It is a love directed toward others, putting the needs of others ahead of oneself. This is the kind of love people saw in Jesus.

When the New Testament declares that "God is love," it means that these two language symbols—*God* and *love*—are identical. If God is love, then the converse is also true: love is God. Therefore, the word "God" is a name we give to the spirit of selfless love found at the depths of our humanity and experienced in the relationship of self-giving human love toward one another. Thus, "God" can be

6. 1 John 4:16.

7. John 4: 24: "God is spirit, and those who worship him must worship in spirit and truth."

8. 1 John 1:5: "God is light and in him there is no darkness at all."

9. 1 John 4:7–8: "Beloved, let us love one another, because love is from God; everyone who loves is born of God and knows God. Whoever does not love does not know God, for God is love."

seen as a language symbol that personifies self-giving compassionate love as a divine entity. For millennia, humans have projected this image of God onto a supernatural being. However, according to the First Letter of John, God is not a loving being. God is love itself.

## DWELLING IN HUMANITY

Love, bound up in human flesh, is the manifestation of God in the world. This is another way of looking at divine incarnation. For the early church, Jesus embodied the image of a God of love, revealed in his words and deeds. Therefore, some saw him as the incarnation of God on earth.

However, the radical message of the New Testament is that God is no longer an external being who dwells in heaven; God has come to dwell among us, not just in the person of Jesus, but within every human being.[10] Indeed, God has always—and only—been a part of humanity, located deep within human consciousness and projected as a divine actor in the human story. God, in the form of compassionate love, is a latent presence within each of us, but this God remains hidden until humans outwardly express love toward others. Loving one another is the full expression of God on earth.[11]

Further, I do not believe that one must be a Christian to be engaged in the work of the conspiracy of love. After all, the peasants Jesus spoke to in Galilee, Judea, and Samaria were not Christians, and they were the first ones called to the task. The Jewish concept of *tikkun olam*, a Hebrew phrase that means repairing or healing the world, likewise suggests that as humans we have a shared responsibility to transform the world through social action in the pursuit of justice and peace. Many other faiths have similar calls to work for a better world. The vision of Jesus requires the involvement of people everywhere—people of every faith and

10. John 1:14, "The logos became flesh and pitched a tent among us."

11. 1 John 4:12: "No one has ever seen God. But if we love each other, God lives in us, and His love is brought to full expression in us." (NLT).

people of no faith at all—to make it a reality. The conspiracy of love feels right at home in the secular world.

German pastor, theologian, and martyr Dietrich Bonhoeffer (1906–1945) wrote from prison in May 1944:

> *The day will come . . . when people will once more be called to speak the word of God in such a way that the world is changed and renewed. It will be in a new language, perhaps quite nonreligious language, but liberating and redeeming like Jesus's language, so that people will be alarmed, and yet overcome by its power—the language of a new righteousness and truth, a language proclaiming that God makes peace with humankind and that God's kingdom is drawing near.*[12]

So, *the conspiracy of love* is my suggested metaphor for the kingdom of God. It may not be perfect, but I believe it is a phrase that is well suited for the postmodern world and may have an appeal to younger generations. I will use it interchangeably with *the kingdom of God* throughout this book.

12. Bonhoeffer, *Letters and Papers*, 300.

CHAPTER 2

# THE PERSISTENT WIDOW / THE FRIEND AT MIDNIGHT

*You just need to be a flea against injustice.*
*Enough committed fleas biting strategically*
*can make even the biggest dog uncomfortable*
*and transform even the biggest nation.*

—MARIAN WRIGHT EDELMAN (B. 1939)

IN A LATE-NIGHT SESSION on February 7, 2017, during Jeff Sessions' (b. 1946) confirmation hearing for U.S. Attorney General, just weeks after the inauguration of President Donald Trump (b. 1946), the United States Senate voted to silence Senator Elizabeth Warren (b. 1949) after she read comments made decades earlier by Edward Kennedy and Coretta Scott King that criticized the civil rights record of Senator Jefferson Beauregard Sessions III. Warren was censured because Senate Rule XIX prohibits ascribing "to another senator or to other senators any conduct or motive unworthy or unbecoming a senator." To silence her, Senate Majority Leader Mitch McConnell (b. 1942) led a party-line vote that forced Senator Warren to take her seat and refrain from speaking. McConnell later said "Senator Warren was giving a lengthy speech. She had appeared to violate the rule. She was warned. She was given an explanation. Nevertheless, she persisted."

That phrase, "Nevertheless, she persisted," became a rallying cry for the women's movement that had been ignited by the election of Donald Trump. Writer Valerie Schultz (b. 1965) wrote in a religious journal,[1] "It is a phrase we women embrace because persistence is what we do."

> *We women persist. Isn't that our job? Throughout history, we have persisted in our quest for respect, for justice, for equal rights, for suffrage, for education, for enfranchisement, for recognition, for making our voices heard. In the face of violence, of opposition, of ridicule, of belittlement, even of jail time, nevertheless, we have persisted.*[2]

## THE PERSISTENT WIDOW

In the parable sometimes called "The Unjust Judge" but more accurately titled "The Persistent Widow," Jesus tells the story of a woman who persisted and persevered. Usually, the parable is interpreted as an allegory about prayer and that is the way Luke's gospel presents it.

> *Then Jesus told them a parable about their need to pray always and not to lose heart.*
>
> *In a certain city there was a certain judge who did not fear God and who did not care about people. In that same city, there was a widow who kept coming to him and demanding, "Give me justice against my opponent." For some time, he refused. But finally, he said to himself, "Even though I don't fear God or care about people, yet because this widow keeps bothering me, I'm going to give her a favorable ruling, or else she'll keep coming back until she wears me down!"*[3]

1. *America: the Jesuit Review of Faith & Culture.*
2. Schultz, *America.*
3. Luke 18:1–5.

In his conclusion, Luke makes a comparison of the lesser to the greater. He has Jesus say to his listeners that if an unjust judge can become worn down by repeated pleas for justice, then do not lose heart if God seems immune to your prayers. Just keep praying.

> And the Lord [Jesus] said, 'Listen to what the unjust judge says. And will not God grant justice to his chosen ones who cry to him day and night? Will he delay long in helping them? I tell you, he will quickly grant justice to them.[4]

Yet, as David Buttrick (1927–2017), a professor of homiletics at the Vanderbilt University Divinity School, once wrote, "The notion that, repeatedly, we must bang on the doors of heaven to catch God's attention is hardly an appropriate theology of prayer."[5] There is much more going on in this parable than prayer.

Parables are not allegories. The characters do not stand for someone else. The judge is not God. The widow is not us—although, of the two characters, she is the one we most identify with. Rather, a parable is an imaginative metaphor in story form that is meant to startle us, to raise questions, and to challenge our conventional thinking. This is not an allegory about prayer; it is a tale about a flea biting a dog.

This is a spare tale, without much detail or background on the characters. We are told that the judge dwells in a city and thus may be a member of the urban elite. Nothing apparently shames him—neither God nor other people. Tradition characterizes him as unjust, but the parable itself does not state that, although Luke's conclusion does. We are not told that the judge accepts bribes or is partial to the wealthy, though both of those may be true. The legal system of any domination society is rarely a guarantor of justice to powerless, marginalized people. It is tilted toward the elites in society.

---

4. Luke 18:6–8.
5. Buttrick, *Speaking Parables*, 186.

## THE JUDGE

First, consider the character of the judge. We have recently found out about some apparently corrupt conservative justices of the U.S. Supreme Court and their love of money. It is all over the news as I write. Justice Clarence Thomas (b. 1948) regularly accepted lavish gifts worth hundreds of thousands of dollars from Republican billionaire Harlan Crow (b. 1949). His benefactor paid for private jets, luxury trips, family property, and had also secretly paid the private school tuition for Thomas's grandnephew who he was raising as a son. None of this was declared on Thomas' financial disclosure forms, which is against the law. It was later revealed that a $276,000 motor home was apparently bought by another friend. Then, it was revealed that Justice Thomas accepted at least 38 vacations, 26 private jet flights, eight flights by helicopter, a dozen VIP passes to sporting events, as well as stays at luxury resorts in Florida and Jamaica. None of this was declared. His wife Virginia 'Ginni' Thomas (b. 1957) accepted cash payments from Leonard Leo (b. 1967), the longtime vice-president of the Federalist Society[6] that backs originalist judges and has been key to transforming the federal judiciary. He surreptitiously funneled tens of thousands of dollars to Ginni for "consulting work" a decade ago. Thomas never declared this as joint income either. Justice Samuel Alito (b. 1950) also accepted at least one luxury vacation at a fishing lodge including private air travel from Paul Singer (b. 1944), a Republican hedge-fund billionaire who has repeatedly asked the Supreme Court to rule in his favor in high-stakes business disputes. Alito did not report the trip and did not recuse himself from those cases involving his benefactor. Justice Neil Gorsuch (b. 1967) benefitted from a real estate deal but neglected to disclose that the buyer was Brian Duffy (b. 1965), the head of Greenberg Traurig, one of the nation's biggest law firms with a robust practice

---

6. The Federalist Society for Law and Public Policy Studies is an American conservative and libertarian legal organization that advocates for a textualist and originalist interpretation of the U.S. Constitution. It was founded in 1982. They have recently published *Project 2025*, a radical call for the dismantling of American government.

before the high court. And the wife of Chief Justice John Roberts (b. 1955), Jane Sullivan Roberts (b. 1950), has made millions of dollars as a legal recruiter, placing lawyers at firms with business before the Supreme Court. In June 2023, Justice Alito complained to *The Wall Street Journal* that he did not like the way the court's legitimacy was being questioned. "We are being hammered daily." Hammered for apparent partiality and openness to bribery involving wealthy conservative elites.

## THE WIDOW

Now consider the widow. She is often a powerless person in first-century Jewish society, no longer having a male protector in a patriarchal system. The Torah regularly states that three groups of people fall under God's special care—widows, orphans, and resident aliens—because they have no male or clan protectors. According to Deuteronomy:

> *For Yahweh your God is God of gods and Lord of lords, the great God, mighty and awesome, who is not partial and takes no bribe, who executes justice for the orphan and the widow, and who loves the strangers, providing them with food and clothing.*[7]

> *Cursed be anyone who deprives the alien, the orphan, and the widow of justice.*[8]

So, the widow seeks justice, and one would have to believe from the Hebrew Bible that God is on her side. We don't know if this particular widow is young or old, but she lives in a time when few lived beyond the age of thirty-five except for the very wealthy. We don't know whether she is rich or poor. If she too is a city-dweller, then she is most likely not a subsistence farmer like the majority of peasants. She has the luxury of spending time pestering the judge, which is not something many poor people can do while trying to survive. We are told that she keeps coming and

7. Deut 10:17–18.
8. Deut 27:19.

coming, but does that mean she is continually coming to the court, or does she also approach the judge in the synagogue, on the street, or at his home? Her behavior would be considered shameless and brazen in that culture. She may be weak, but she is clearly not helpless. She is feisty and tenacious. And she has the audacity and persistence to continually harass the judge for the justice she desires.

We don't know what the legal matter is all about. Is someone trying to take advantage of her? Is it about inheritance or a land dispute? All we know is that she is seeking justice or vindication.

## PERSISTENT STRUGGLE

And the judge finally gives in to her persistence. She simply wears him down. Like Justice Alito, he is tired of being hammered daily. The Greek verb translated as "wear me down" is actually a boxing term meaning to "beat me up," "give me a black eye," or "beat me black and blue." The judge probably means this metaphorically rather than literally. He is simply tired of the persistent demand and so he gives in. When the widow gets justice, it is only because she would not retreat, she would not back down, and she would not give up the fight. She was determined to get what she came for.

The parable is not about prayer. It is about persistence. It is about not accepting being ignored or rebuffed or overlooked or silenced. It is about struggling against a system that is at best indifferent, and where the law is frequently unjust to the marginalized.

Scholar Bernard Brandon Scott (b. 1941) says that this persistent struggle is a viable metaphor for the kingdom of God:

> *The kingdom keeps coming, keeps battering down regardless of honor or justice. It may even come under the guise of shamelessness.*[9]

This is a story about kingdom tactics. Powerless people must keep striving for justice until the system gives in, because, as Frederick Douglass (1818–1895) said:

---

9. Scott, *Hear Then the Parable*, 187.

*Power concedes nothing without a demand. It never has and it never will.*[10]

New Testament scholar and farmer Clarence Jordan (1912–1969) commented on this parable in this way:

> *There are times when causing trouble is the witness we must raise for the sake of justice. There are times when the depth of our concern for something will cause us to over-step the bounds of a common law and order for the sake of a higher law and order. I do not believe that Jesus wants us to literally bruise the body politic, but Jesus uses strong language to make his point: what is just in God's eyes is more important than standard operating procedure in the eyes of our culture.*[11]

If an allegory is needed to help explain the parable, then do not look for God in the role of the indifferent judge. Rather, God should be seen in the character of the persistent widow, always seeking justice. That is more likely to be where God is found in the struggle between justice and the law.

## THE FRIEND AT MIDNIGHT

Another parable of persistence that Jesus told is that of the friend at midnight.

> *Suppose one of you has a friend, and you go to him at midnight and say to him, "Friend, lend me three loaves of bread; for a friend of mine has arrived, and I have noth-ing to set before him." And he answers from within, "Do not bother me; the door has already been locked, and my children are with me in bed; I cannot get up and give you anything." I tell you, even though he will not get up and give him anything because he is his friend, at least because*

---

10. Douglass, from a speech delivered on August 3, 1857, at Canandaigua, NY.

11. Jordan, *Cotton Patch Parables of Liberation*, 83.

*of his persistence he will get up and give him whatever he needs.*[12]

This parable presumes a closely-built village in the country-side where at least once a week the village women bake loaves at a communal oven. The peasants who live here are very poor, many living from "hand to mouth." For the protagonist peasant that is literally true. At the end of the day his breadbasket is completely empty. But the people in the village are aware of who has something in their house—a little extra. We are not told these details in this sparse tale; they are presumably taken for granted by Jesus' listeners.

An unexpected visitor arrives in the middle of the night, and according to the law of hospitality, must be offered a meal. In the tradition of Middle Eastern hospitality, a guest is entitled to more than a place to sleep, but also must be served a meal, given the best that one has, and afforded whatever aid is necessary. This is true not only for the host but also for the host's connections in the village. They must respond or suffer a loss of honor.

The house belonging to the host's friend, like nearly all the houses in the village, is likely small and simple. It contains a single room for living, eating, and sleeping. The room has no windows and a door that is barred with a sturdy beam passed between two iron rings. The friend has long ago gone to bed with the arrival of darkness, sleeping on the floor with his wife and children.

So, the host in need of bread walks to his friend's house and begins banging on the door.

> *"Friend, lend me three loaves of bread; for a friend of mine has arrived, and I have nothing to set before him." And he answers from within, "Do not bother me; the door has already been locked, and my children are with me in bed; I cannot get up and give you anything."*

Yet, he eventually gives in because of the host's noisy persistence. Not just because he is a friend, but because he wants to shut

---

12. Luke 11:5–8.

him up before he arouses others in the village. The host's raucous and shameless behavior is disturbing the peace.

This parable counters the narrative of a dog-eat-dog society, where people refused to help one another in the face of desperate circumstances. Those who had more, simply congratulated themselves, closed their eyes, ears, and hearts, and were indifferent to the needs of those who had less. It was an oppressive and unjust social order with no system of communal support for those who suffered the most. The Judean and Galilean cultures exhibited a disregard of the ancient covenant of a contrast society. There was no commitment to the common good, no obligation to being one's brothers or sisters keeper. But friendship counted for something, and Jesus is proposing that helping one another, even when it discomforts us, is the right way to act. It may require persistence and shameless behavior to rouse us but is the right thing to do.

Congressman John Lewis (1940–2020) reflecting on the life and legacy of civil rights leader Rosa Parks (1913–2005) said:

> *Rosa Parks inspired us to get in trouble. And I've been getting in trouble ever since. She inspired us to find a way, to get in the way, to get in what I call good trouble, necessary trouble. She kept on saying to each one of us, you too can do something. If you see something that is not right, not fair, not just: do something. We cannot afford to be quiet.*

We are called to become persistent troublemakers and disturbers of the peace on behalf of the conspiracy of love for social justice. As French theologian Jacques Ellul (1912–1994) wrote:

> *Christians were never meant to be normal. We've always been holy troublemakers, we've always been creators of uncertainty, agents of a dimension that's incompatible with the status quo; we do not accept the world as it is, but we insist on the world becoming the way that God wants it to be. And the Kingdom of God is different from the patterns of this world.*[13]

---

13. This popular quote is attributed to Ellul, but I have not been able to verify its source. But from my reading of Ellul, it sounds very characteristic of him.

# CHAPTER 3

# THE MUSTARD SEED AND THE LEAVEN

*We must let go of the life we have planned,*
*so as to accept the one that is waiting for us.*

—JOSEPH CAMPBELL (1904–1987)

THE THRUST OF THE parables is often to subvert the distorted myths in which people live their lives. A myth is what holds many people's lives together. In some cases, our myths are an attempt to resolve the tensions of everyday life by promising an idealized future in which one will be rescued from all the problems of ordinary life. And sometimes the myths are about the past, glorifying participants in great victories or defeats.

## AMERICAN MYTHS

For instance, law professor Michel Paradis (b. 1980), writing about the myth of the Southern Lost Cause, said:

> *The Lost Cause recast the Confederacy's humiliating defeat in a treasonous war for slavery as the embodiment of the Framers' true vision for America. Supporters pushed the*

*ideas that the Civil War was not actually about slavery; that Robert E. Lee was a brilliant general, gentleman, and patriot; and that the Ku Klux Klan had rescued the heritage of the old South, what came to be known as "the southern way of life."[1]*

Then on January 6, 2021, following the defeat of Donald Trump (b. 1946) in the 2020 election, a violent mob of his supporters attacked the United States Capitol Building in Washington, DC. The mob was seeking to keep Trump in power by preventing a joint session of Congress from the ceremonial counting of electoral college votes to formalize the victory of President-elect Joe Biden (b. 1942). More than 2,000 insurrectionists stormed the building and occupied, vandalized, and looted it. They assaulted Capitol Police officers and attempted to locate key lawmakers to capture and harm them. With building security breached, Capitol Police evacuated legislators and locked down both chambers of Congress and several buildings in the Capitol Complex. Insurrectionists occupied the empty Senate chamber while federal law enforcement officers defended the evacuated House floor. More than 140 police officers reported suffering injuries. Seven people died as a result of that attempted coup.

The Capitol was finally cleared of rioters by mid-evening, and the counting of the electoral votes resumed. The official count was further delayed when co-conspirators in both houses of Congress attempted to challenge the vote counts of various states. The count was eventually completed in the early morning hours of January 7.

The many millions who watched the events unfold that day on their televisions instantly knew that it would rank among the most anguished and horrifying days in American history. But it was worse and more wretched than we imagined. Thanks to the exceptional work of the House Select Committee that investigated the January 6 attacks, we now know the details of a deliberate, coordinated, violent, multipart plan to overturn the 2020 presidential election. And the main actor was the nation's president. "The central cause of January 6 was one man—former President

1. Paradis, "Lost Cause's Legacy," *Atlantic*.

Donald Trump—whom many others followed," the report of the committee said. "None of the events of January 6 would have happened without him."

The attack on the Capitol was unmistakably an act of political violence, not merely an exercise in vandalism or trespassing amid a disorderly protest that had spiraled out of control. Writing in *The Atlantic* magazine, David A. Graham (b. 1983) described how pro-Trump factions are now trying to redefine January 6 as a mythic symbol, a "New Lost Cause."[2] The New Lost Cause, like the old one, seeks to convert a shameful catastrophe into a celebration of the heroism and honor of the culprits and portray those who attacked the country as the true patriots.

The problem with these myths, the Lost Cause and the New Lost Cause, is that they emphasize the supposed valor of the people involved, while whitewashing what they were actually doing. The January 6 insurrectionists violently assaulted the seat of American government. They do not deserve revisionist celebration.

## THE MYTHICAL VISION OF ISRAEL

For the people of Jesus' time, the tension between everyday reality and a mythical vision of Israel as God's chosen people was felt with particular urgency. From the heyday of national power and prestige during the reigns of King David (reign c, 1000–970 BCE) and King Solomon (reign 970–931 BCE), Israel had been on a downhill slide for several centuries, its kingdom conquered and divided several times over. The Jewish people looked forward to the day when God would act to reverse this trend. The Day of Yahweh, when it came, would introduce a glorious new age of universal peace, with God's chosen people at the head of the nations. In the particular myth in which the people of first-century Israel were living, the establishment of God's rule had specific connotations of power, triumph, holiness, and grandeur.

---

2. Graham, "New Lost Cause," *Atlantic*.

The cultural symbol for this myth were the great cedars of Lebanon, comparable to the huge redwood trees of California. They grew straight up for two or three hundred feet or more. Every kind of bird could nest in their branches and enjoy their shade. This image was deeply embedded in the cultural conditioning of the Jewish people. From their defeat they would become the greatest of all nations just as the great cedar of Lebanon was the greatest of all trees.

In the words of the prophet Ezekiel:

> Consider . . . a cedar of Lebanon, with fair branches and forest shade, and of great height, its top among the clouds . . . it towered high above all the trees of the field; its boughs grew large and its branches long . . . All the birds of the air made their nests in its boughs; under its branches all the animals of the field gave birth to their young; and in its shade all great nations lived.[3]

## A MUSTARD SEED

Instead, Jesus proposed this parable:

> What is the kingdom of God like? What does it remind me of? It is like a mustard seed that someone took and tossed in the garden. It grew and became a tree, and the birds of the sky roosted in its branches.[4]

There are four versions of this parable found in the gospels of Matthew, Mark, Luke, and Thomas, a document recovered about seventy-five years ago in the Nag Hammadi Gnostic collection, which many scholars think is closer in some places to the original oral tradition. In Luke's gospel he says the seed is tossed in a garden. The others say it is thrown on the ground, on prepared soil, and in a field. I'll address Luke's suggested garden as the scene of the crime.

3. Ezek 31:3, 5–6.
4. Luke 13:18–19.

For an alert hearer of Jesus' day, the detail about the garden would be a tip-off. In the Jewish view of the world, order was identified with holiness and disorder with impurity. Hence, there were very strict rules about what could be planted in a household garden. The rabbinical law of mixtures or "diverse kinds" ruled that one could not mix certain plants in the same garden or field, just as one could not mix fabrics such as wool and linen in clothing, or the crossbreeding of animals in farming, or the marriage of a pure Israelite to someone whose bloodline was suspect. The law was intended to maintain order in a disorderly world, and in the case of marriage to maintain the ideal of racial purity.

The mustard plant was forbidden in a household garden because it was fast spreading and would surely invade the vegetables. In stating that this person threw a mustard seed in a garden, the hearers are alerted to the fact that he or she was doing something illegal or impure. An unclean image thus becomes the starting point for Jesus' vision of the kingdom of God in this parable.

If the starting point is an unclean image, the rest of the parable becomes even more perplexing. What do we know about the mustard plant, botanically speaking? The mustard plant is just one step ahead of being an ordinary weed. It is a common, fast-spreading shrub, which grows to about three to four feet in height and is adorned with pretty yellow flowers. It puts out a few branches. No self-respecting bird would build a nest in this puny shrub. At best, a few birds might rest in its shade.

For Luke and Matthew, contrary to all botanical good sense, the mustard seed does in fact turn into a tree. In Mark, the earliest gospel, it turns into the greatest of shrubs. In Thomas, even earlier, it turns into a great branch so that many birds can rest in its shade. All of these expectations are contrary to the facts. A mustard seed does not become a tree or the greatest of shrubs, nor put forth a great branch, however much one may want it to.

Steeped in their cultural image of the great cedars of Lebanon, the hearers might be expecting the tiny mustard seed to grow into a mighty tree. Jesus' point is exactly the opposite. It just becomes an invasive shrub, and a few birds might rest under its modest branches. That's all. The image of the kingdom of God as a towering cedar of Lebanon is subverted by Jesus. Once again, his listeners are frustrated. The parable subverts all the grandiose ideas about what the kingdom is going to be like when it arrives in its fulness.

One of the most firmly held Israelite expectations was that the Day of Yahweh would manifest the final triumph of God in history. Its arrival, heralded by a long-awaited Messiah, would rescue Israel from its miserable subservience to the Roman Empire. It was a future event, not one firmly rooted in the here-and-now. Jesus proclaimed the alternative Kingdom of God in contrast to the more widely used phrase the Day of Yahweh (or the Day of the Lord as it is usually translated in English Bibles). That is because they offer two different views about God's action in the world.

The kingdom, according to Jesus, will not fulfill our expectations. It is not something great and glorious. It will not arrive with fanfare and trumpets. It will simply appear in the midst of ordinary life. And to most people it will be so insignificant that they will not even notice its presence other that this pungent weed seems to be spreading everywhere. In this parable, Jesus shows us that we do not have to wait for an apocalyptic deliverance. We do not have to wait for a grandiose liberation. The kingdom is available right now. It is here in our midst, and we do not even realize it.

## THE MYTH RECAPTURES THE PARABLE

So difficult was it for people of Jesus' time to get over their idea of the kingdom of God as a triumphant institution that even the gospel writers tried to change it into something great anyway. In other words, the myth recaptured the parable. The parable was meant to subvert one's idea about the kingdom, but what happened was that the old mindset began to interpret the parable in a way that was consistent with its former mythical expectations. The oral tradition was evidently influenced by the old expectations of grandeur as people gradually slipped back into their former mindsets.

If we are looking for a great expansion of our particular re-ligion, nation, ethnic group, or social movement into some great visible organization that rules the earth, we are on the wrong track. According to Jesus, this is not God's idea of success.

## DISTURBING THE SOCIAL ORDER

Instead of vertical growth like a cedar tree, Jesus proposes a hori-zontal growth, the mustard seed spreading rapidly, infesting the garden. Maybe it meant in its original form that the kingdom of God—the conspiracy of love—profoundly disrupts the social order. Someone performed a prohibited act. Tossing the seed in the garden was an act of disobedience and disorder designed to spoil the pure order of the garden. Was this a conspiratorial act to disturb not only order, but holiness also?

The mustard seed parable challenged the biblical law that two disparate things must not mix. The Jewish people of the first cen-tury were extremely concerned with preserving their racial purity, not mixing their bloodlines with anyone inferior. Do not forget that apartheid in South Africa and racial segregation in the U.S. were legal systems that opposed the mixing of people in suppos-edly ordered societies. Intermarriage between the races was illegal. This parable may be seen as an act of protest and defiance toward these racial restrictions.

The kingdom is not concerned with righteous people's idea of religious purity or cleanliness. It is meant for the poor, the unkempt, the unclean, and the outcast. And it is all around us, spreading out of control.

## YEAST / LEAVEN

*He told them another parable: "The kingdom of God is like yeast that a woman took and concealed in fifty pounds of flour until all of it was leavened."*[5]

5. Luke 13:20–21.

Modern people often think of leaven in a positive sense—as fermentation, new life, and growth. But for the people of Israel, leaven—today's yeast—was a sign of uncleanness and corruption. Leavened bread was the symbol of the unholy, the profane, a sign of everyday life. The Bible often uses "yeast" or "leaven" to signify anything which rots and corrupts, not just physically but spiritually and morally as well. Jesus reportedly warned his disciples against being taken in by the teachings of both the Pharisees and the Sadducees, which he compared to leaven.

*Beware of the leaven of the Pharisees and Sadducees.*[6]

In ancient times, leaven was made by mixing wheat flour and water into a paste or dough and setting the mixture in a damp, dark place for several days. Wild yeast is a naturally occurring living organism. It lives on the wheat plant, so that the yeast from the ground grain, combined with yeast spores from the air, will begin a process of fermentation. The combination feeds on sugars that are naturally present in the flour, releasing carbon dioxide in the process. These bubbles of gas cause the dough to rise. The dough is now an active leaven starter. When mixed into a new batch of dough, bubbles created by the microbes in the starter will cause the dough to expand and increase in size. When the dough is baked, the yeast dies and the air pockets set, giving the baked product a soft and spongy appearance.

Unleavened bread was the symbol of the holy and sacred. The Feast of Unleavened Bread—a seven-day celebration—commemorates the biblical story of the Israelites' escape from 400-years of Egyptian slavery. It reminds Israel they had to flee Egypt hurriedly. They could not wait for their daily bread to rise, so they brought unleavened or flat bread with them.

The large amount of flour in this parable was actually three *se'im* (SAY-im), the plural form of one *se'ah* (SAY-ah) which was a Hebrew unit of dry volume equal to about seven quarts. Three se'im is therefore equivalent to 21 quarts or 5.25 gallons. It is enough flour to make bread for a great feast. It is the same amount

6. Matt 16:6.

that Sarah used to make bread for the three men/angels who visited Abraham who was camping at the Oaks of Mamre.[7] Upon the stranger's arrival, Abraham rushed into the tent and said to Sarah, "Make ready quickly three measures (se'im) of fine meal, knead it, and make loaves." In the tale, one of the visitors (who was actually Yahweh in person) foretold the birth of Isaac to aging Sarah and Abraham. Abraham soon realized that Yahweh's unexpected appearance at Mamre was an epiphany or sudden manifestation of his presence. So, through the parable of the rising bread dough, Jesus' listeners might have been expecting an epiphany—a sudden moment of revelation and insight—to occur.

Although many translations of this parable suggested the woman "mixed in" or "kneaded in" the leaven, a more accurate translation would be that she actually "hid" or "concealed" the leaven into the dough, a conspiratorial action leading to massive transformation. In time, the whole batch becomes leavened—thoroughly unclean and corrupt. Jesus paints a vision of God working to transform the world from within.

## THE RABBLE WHO FOLLOWED JESUS

The parable suggests that the kingdom of God will not take place where people are concerned about remaining holy and uncorrupted by the world. Reaching out in love, compassion, reconciliation, and forgiveness is more important in Jesus' eyes than moral purity. Also, and most importantly, the kingdom of God is made up of people who the world views as sinful, immoral, and dishonest. The social category called the "sinners" are the poorest of the poor: unclean, dirty, hungry, and willing to do almost anything to survive. They included prostitutes, gamblers, swindlers, and corrupt tax officials.

The followers of Jesus did not obey the oral laws and prohibitions of the Pharisees. They included the "*am ha'aretz*" (*ahm hah-AHR-etz*) or "the people of the land"—uneducated people,

---

7. Gen 18:1–19.

who were negligent in their observance of all 613 *mitzvot*, laws or commandments in the Torah, due to their ignorance. The nearest English equivalent is "ignorant rubes." They made up the rabble who followed Jesus. He called them his brothers and sisters.

In the following sayings, Jesus refers to the "poor" with the Greek word *ptóchos (pto-KHOS)*, which does not mean the working poor, but instead those in wretched poverty, the miserable beggars on the streets, those who have lost everything and are without hope. It is translated literally as "one who crouches and cowers."

> *The spirit of Yahweh is upon me, because he has anointed me to bring good news to the poor [ptóchos]. He has sent me to proclaim release to the captives and recovery of sight to the blind, to let the oppressed go free, to proclaim the year of Yahweh's favor.*[8]
>
> *Blessed are you who are poor [ptóchos], for yours is the kingdom of God. Blessed are you who are hungry now, for you will be filled. Blessed are you who weep now, for you will laugh.*[9]

This is a radical idea. Beggars, the wretched poor, prostitutes, and corrupt officials are inheritors and inhabitants of the kingdom of God. Not the wealthy. Not the religious. Not the good or holy people. But "sinners" and the poor. Jesus said to the chief priests and the elders, who were the lay aristocracy, "I swear to you, the tax-collectors and the prostitutes will get into the kingdom of God, but you will not." In this parable, Jesus again confronts the popular idea that the kingdom of God is both holy and good.

The leaven itself is not visible in the dough, but the effect of its action is gradually noticeable, sometimes taking us by surprise. We are left with the hope of revolutionary transformation without any experience of it happening. The kingdom is active when we join with the poor, hungry, and seemingly immoral people and turn our backs on domination, greed, power, and violence. It is found when we begin to live out God's vision of acceptance, compassion, sharing, and reconciliation.

8. Luke 4:18–19.

9. Luke 6:20–21.

## VISION OF A NEW COMMUNITY

Rather than the restoration of political and religious power through external action, Jesus painted a vision of God changing the world from within, through the creation of a new society bonded together through new social relationships. Jesus described what would happen when God finally broke through the hearts and minds of people to transform their actions and relationships into a community based on equity and inclusion. He proclaimed that the kingdom had already arrived and could be entered into if a person underwent a radical transformation of inclusion, acceptance, and compassion. This is easier for the poor than it is for the righteous and the wealthy.

The kingdom of God, according to the parables of Jesus, is largely hidden from the world, like an underground conspiracy. It is found in lives that are transformed. Christians today, especially in conservative churches, try to do the same thing the Pharisees did: keep themselves holy by maintaining separation from those they deem sinful. The category of sinful people varies, but usually includes LGBTQ+ people. These conservatives regularly tell the "sinners" that they can only be accepted if they give up their sexual orientation and turn their backs on their "sinful" ways. In other words, they must appear to be straight and deny their true selves to be accepted. These conservative Christians are all for transformation, but in their minds, it is others who must be transformed, not them.

But Jesus calls for a different kind of transformation. Not in moving from sinfulness to righteousness, but instead moving from moral segregation to inclusion without any repentance required whatsoever. True religion is found when we reject respectability, holiness, and piety, instead getting our hands dirty, blending our lives with the poor, sick, and unclean, and welcoming the despised and unloved. True religion is not found in religious rituals, beliefs, and moral codes but in loving human relationships and compassionate service to others. It is found in the acceptance of all people and in the recognition of their dignity. Care for the lost and lonely, compassion for the poor and destitute, and love for all, are signs of the presence of the kingdom—the conspiracy of love.

Following Jesus is a response to his call to transform and renew society. It is a summons to be an agent of change, or as Jesus said, to be like a mustard seed in a tidy garden, a pinch of yeast in a large bowl of bread dough, a dash of salt in a pot of soup, or a small lamp in a darkened room. It is to conspire with others so that little by little, a violent, hungry, and suffering world can be renewed for the sake of its children. We become like mustard seeds and leaven when we join in a conspiracy of love to transform ourselves and our society at the local, national, and global levels.

# CHAPTER 4

# THE WORKERS IN THE VINEYARD

*I cook with wine. Sometimes I even add it to the food.*
—W. C. Fields (1880–1946)

Jesus told his disciples this parable:

> The kingdom of heaven[1] [the kingdom of God] is like a
> landowner who went out early in the morning, around
> 6 o'clock, to hire laborers for his vineyard. After agreeing
> with the laborers for the usual daily wage of one denarius,
> he sent them into his vineyard.
>
> When he went out about nine o'clock, he saw others
> standing idle in the marketplace; and he said to them,
> "You also go into the vineyard, and I will pay you whatever
> is right." So, they went.
>
> When he went out again about noon and about three
> o'clock, he did the same.
>
> And about five o'clock he went out and found oth-
> ers standing around; and he said to them, "Why are you

1. Matthew's term "the kingdom of heaven" has caused much confusion
over the years. It is a substitute for "the kingdom of God," which was the authentic term used by Jesus. Matthew was writing for a community of Jewish
Christians for whom taking the Lord's name in vain was a real issue.

*standing here idle all day?" They said to him, "Because no one has hired us." He said to them, "You also go into the vineyard."*

*Around 6 o'clock, when evening came, the lord of the vineyard said to his foreman, "Call the laborers and give them their pay, beginning with the last and then going to the first."*

*When those hired about five o'clock came, each of them received the usual daily wage of one denarius. Now when the first came, they thought they would receive more for their twelve hours of labor; but each of them also received the usual daily wage. And when they received it, they grumbled against the landowner, saying, "These last worked only one hour, and you have made them equal to us who have borne the burden of the day and the scorching heat."*

*But he replied to the ringleader, "Friend, I am not cheating you. Did you not make an agreement with me for one denarius? Take your denarius and go! I wish to give to this last one the same as I give to you. Is it not permissible to do what I wish with the things that are mine? Or are you envious because I am generous?"[2]*

## HISTORICAL CONTEXT

Knowing the historical context in which this parable was told can lead to some unusual and even disturbing conclusions about its meaning. In first-century Palestine, work was scarce and poverty widespread. Day laborers were peasants who had lost their land through indebtedness. If they were no longer needed as tenant farmers for the new landowners, they would become part of the "expendable" class. They were on a downward spiral and were desperate for work to survive. They did not have many options. They could choose between day labor or robbery. If they were too weak for either of these, they would become beggars at the gate, like

2. Matt 20:1–16.

Lazarus,[3] until they died of hunger and disease. When Thomas Hobbes (1588–1679), reflecting on the fate of peasants in a time of war, said that the life of humanity was "solitary, poor, nasty, brutish, and short," it could aptly apply to the expendable class in the time of Jesus.

In this tale, Jesus brings together the social extremes of an agrarian society: the wealthy elites and the expendables. And he arranges this meeting at a time when the elites were dependent on the lowliest of laborers. To ensure a timely harvest, the landowner needed their labor.

Small peasant farmers would often have a small vineyard for their own needs, but this parable is about the owner of a large vineyard estate. Wealthy elites could only create large estates by foreclosing on the land of indebted peasants, joining lot to lot. Only the wealthy could afford to create a large vineyard because it could take up to four years to get the first usable crop. Vineyards provided a cash crop to sustain the elites' lifestyles. Wine was an export product that could be shipped throughout the Roman Empire.

Contrary to most interpretations of this parable, Jesus' audience would probably not associate a wealthy landowner with God. Peasants found nothing good, righteous, or holy about rich land barons. For some reason, we moderns assume that the rich man or the king always represents God in a parable. We tend to idealize the superior and wealthy character giving them the benefit of the doubt as to the source of their wealth. But peasants had no love for the elite class. And the estate managers, stewards, or foremen—although usually arising from the peasant class—were not trusted or respected either. They were considered complicit in the exploitation of the poor.

3. Luke 16:19–31.

## USUAL DAILY WAGE

Many translations of this parable substitute the phrase "the usual daily wage" for the Greek "a denarius for the day." I suppose this is to ease the comprehension of modern readers who have no idea about the value of a silver denarius coin in the first century relative to our times. One denarius a day—the daily wage in this parable—was not enough to support a large family. A single individual could stay alive on about a half denarius per day, but only survive. This much is certain—the landowner is not being generous in the wages he pays.

To give us a modern comparison, an unskilled day laborer can make about $8 to $10 per hour in the United States today, depending on the market. An agricultural worker in Michigan, where I live, makes about $10 an hour. In 2024, the official minimum wage was $10.33 per hour. But to be clear, these are poverty wages. Compare that to a *living* wage in Detroit which is $19.65 per hour for a single person. To support a family of four, a laborer would have to make $44.76 per hour.[4] So, let us assume these vineyard workers were making the poverty wage of $10 per hour. For twelve hours of labor (6 AM to 6 PM), this would total about $120 for the day. But let's say that the landowner offered the laborers a $100 daily wage instead of an hourly wage, making the silver denarius coin equivalent to $100 for the sake of discussion.

Note that the vineyard owner does not negotiate the workers' wages. He simply tells the first workers what wage he will pay—the usual daily wage for twelve hours of labor in the hot sun, take it or leave it. After that, he never specifies any wage to the workers at the labor market, except to say that he will pay what is right or just. Again, it is a situation of take it or leave it. For the last workers, he simply says "Go." None of these workers have any choice regarding wages. They have no negotiating power. For day laborers, it is a situation of working for whatever one can get, or quickly starving.

---

4. Living Wage in Wayne County, MI.

## DAY LABORERS

This story presumably takes place during a grape harvest, but it does not specifically state that. A harvest creates an unusual demand for labor. Day laborers, in any age, are never assured of getting work on a regular basis. Work is very spotty. As a result, a day laborer in the first century, with no social safety net, does not have the prospect of a long life. Age, weakness, and disease lead to eventual death in this labor market. The day laborers were most likely all present at the labor market (*agora*) early in the morning. Those picked first are always the fittest—the youngest, healthiest, strongest. Those picked last are the most unfit for hard labor—older, weaker, sickly.

As a youth in St. Louis, the Kingshighway bus route took me north past the Avalon theater, one of two neighborhood movie houses. Day laborers gathered early in the morning at the theater parking lot, which faced the street. As I passed, I would see these shabbily dressed men smoking cigarettes and drinking coffee to stay warm. Occasionally, a pickup truck would pull in and the driver would point to two or three men who would climb in the back. They were going to do yard work or construction work or home demolition. Some were probably skilled in construction; many were most likely unskilled. Years later, I saw the same thing at a small park across from a church in the historic section of Savannah, Georgia. The same downcast look from defeated men. I am told that day laborers often gather today at many Home Depot parking lots across the nation. But I am never up and about early enough to observe the truth of that.

In this parable, those picked last were not slackers. I wish preachers would recognize this. Those last picked did not show up late. They were not spending the early part of the day drinking in a bar. They were simply the most obviously unfit for the task. The parable says clearly that they had been standing there all day, simply because no one selected them.

The landowner curiously has not planned wisely in determining how many workers he needed. He returns four times to hire more workers. Perhaps his concern is to assure the quality of a harvested crop. Grapes had to be picked promptly when ripe or the harvest would be lost. One thing that seems out of character is that the landowner personally hires the workers. Why not have his steward or foreman perform this task? Elites did not usually get involved in this kind of detail.

In the evening, the owner instructs his foreman to assemble the workers. He does not pay them discreetly. This is a public gathering. Normally, we would expect the first hired to be paid first. But this is a set up for a public demonstration of the landowners unquestioned authority. The listening audience to the parable expects justice in payment. They do not receive it.

Let's be clear. The landowner was not being truly generous to anyone in absolute terms. After all, they were poverty wages. It seems that he chooses the last workers to receive their wages first, in order to publicly humiliate the first workers. They each receive a crisp $100 bill. The problem from the point of view of the first picked is that the owner has established the value of their contributions as the same as the last picked. Twelve hour's work or one hour's work, it doesn't matter. The first workers complain, "You have made them equal to us!" When challenged on his behavior, the landowner picks out the ringleader or spokesman of the fittest workers to personally denigrate. He condescendingly calls him "Friend." He delights in saying that he has the power to do whatever he pleases with these men's lives, letting them know in no uncertain terms that they have absolutely no bargaining power with him and no recourse to his decisions. He is the master of their lives and survival.

## ALLEGORIES

Many people have historically interpreted the parables as allegories. An allegory is a story that refers to some other event, person, or thing that is both concealed and revealed in the narration. When taken to an extreme, allegorizing makes every detail symbolic, often investing story elements with unwarranted importance and significance. An allegory uses equal signs. For instance, in an allegorical interpretation: the vineyard = Israel; the landowner = God; the foreman = Jesus; the first workers = the Jews; the last workers = the Christians; or some other scheme for the first and the last (the Jews and the Gentiles, the Pharisees and the outcasts, or lifelong Christians and deathbed converts, for example).

Reading the parables as allegory is a way for the church to domesticate the radical nature of Jesus' teaching. Allegorizing the parables often takes the life out of them. They become dry tales of salvation history rather than stories that invite us in, cause us to think, and take us by surprise. Allegorizing makes the parables safe by substituting unseen characters for known players.

In the nineteenth century, scholars began to react to the allegorization of the parables and suggested that instead these stories were intended to convey just one central concept or idea. They compared Jesus' use of parables to sermon illustrations. The parables did not convey a hidden meaning in every detail, but simply tried to drive home a particular point. In the parable of the workers in the vineyard, Matthew suggests that the point may be that "the last will be first, and the first will be last." However, most preachers today would (and usually do) propose that the point is that God is gracious and generous to all people regardless of merit. However, to buy this point, it is better if we ignore the historical context and its implications.

For many scholars, the parables of Jesus are now being understood to be much more than sermon illustrations, even though the gospel writers themselves often portray them that way. A parable of Jesus stands on its own. It *is* the sermon. The parable *is* the message. Often, it is a message that the listener does not want to hear.

## POETIC METAPHORS OF REVERSAL

More recently, the parables have been talked about as poetic metaphors. Many parables are extended metaphors in narrative form that provide a picture of the kingdom of God. Metaphors often serve the function of explaining something that is completely new or foreign to one's experience, by comparing it to something else within one's frame of reference. It can articulate something that is so alien to one's understanding that no other reference can explain it. The visual imagery of the metaphor invites the listener in to experience the new reality.

So how do we understand this parable in its historic context as an extended metaphor?

First, this is a parable about the kingdom of God, not about God's grace. Jesus begins by saying "The kingdom of Heaven [the kingdom of God] is like a landowner . . ." Parables are not allegories, so the landowner is not God.

Many of Jesus' parables were parables of reversal. In conventional thinking, good people are normally expected to receive good rewards, while bad people are expected to receive bad rewards. This is the nature of justice. But in Jesus' parables, the supposed good people are often denied their expected rewards while the bad, the unclean, the dishonorable, and the undeserving are rewarded. Is that what is happening here? More than any other parable, this one seems to upset the basic structure of an orderly society, the fundamental nature of fairness and justice. It denies equal pay for equal work. Americans believe that reward should be in exact proportion to merit.

In this parable, nobody gets what they expected. The last hired expect only about $10 or so. Certainly, less than a denarius. Instead, they receive the full $100. The first hired, when they see the peculiar generosity of the owner, expect to be paid much more. The last hired are surprised, while the first are incensed. The landowner has insulted them. He has shamed them in public. He has made sure that they know their place.

## WAGES, JUSTICE, AND WORTH

We all know that wages indicate a person's value or worth in a company and in society at-large. This parable subverts the association between wages and worth. It also deals with justice and injustice. Is the goal of justice to ensure that everyone gets what they deserve? Or is it to ensure that everyone is equally accepted as a person of worth?

I'm not sure of the meaning of this parable. The real value of a parable is that its meaning varies among different people. Perhaps the parable is just a lesson about the injustice of the world and the ability of wealthy people to do anything they want. That is Herzog's point. But perhaps there is more.

Maybe it is this. If this is about the kingdom of God, we note that the landowner is constantly calling people to work for him. He is, after all, the real focus of the parable. Like Jesus, he invites them in, regardless of their social value, fitness, or perceived worth. In the end, when the first called—those who think they've worked harder and who expect recognition commensurate with their worth—begin to grumble about being treated equally with those who do less, the landowner tells them to take their wages and go. So, the kingdom of God is like the landowner. How so?

Jesus invites everyone, no matter their status, to enter the kingdom of God and to engage in his conspiracy to work for justice and peace. Within the kingdom, there is no hierarchy. It does not matter if one is giving up everything to treat the dying on the streets of Calcutta or signing online petitions to Congress and writing postcards to voters in one's family room. All workers in God's kingdom are of equal value and worth.

And the work is truly diverse. Many large and small acts are required to help bring about the just, equitable, and compassionate system we are trying to construct here on earth. Some people are needed to build Habitat houses or maintain soup kitchens and clothes closets for the poor. Others may find themselves protesting injustice; getting into "good trouble," as John Lewis used to say. The work may be difficult. The wages will certainly be unfair. The hours may be long. Some may even be beaten, arrested, or jailed. We may never be publicly thanked or get the recognition we think we deserve. But nonetheless, Jesus calls us to labor alongside others in a vast conspiracy of love.

In the first century, Jesus led his small movement in a concerted action to, in John Dominic Crossan's words, subvert the normalcy of civilization and, in Walter Wink's words, to upset the prevailing domination system of society. He called for economic justice, he shared meals with those who were considered outcasts and rabble, he taught creative nonviolent responses to domination, and he led a public demonstration at the seat of political and religious power. He was executed for daring to challenge the status quo that benefited the top one percent of his society.

The way of Jesus may lead to a real cross—an instrument of protracted and painful death. This is not some inward spiritual journey. This is a confrontation with the real world of power, violence, poverty, disease, suffering, and death. But we do not work alone. There are many others walking beside us. The spirit of Jesus leads the way. And he bids us to come and join him in the journey to a better world.

# CHAPTER 5

# THE WIDOW'S MITE

*I wouldn't give you two cents for all your fancy rules if,
behind them, they didn't have a little bit of plain, ordinary,
everyday kindness and a little looking out for the other fella, too.*[1]

—JAMES STEWART (1908–1997)
IN "MR. SMITH GOES TO WASHINGTON"

JESUS WAS IN THE Temple grounds in Jerusalem when he observed
a poor woman.

> *He [Jesus] sat down opposite the treasury and watched
> the crowd putting money into the treasury. Many rich
> people put in large sums. A poor widow came and put in
> two small copper coins, which are worth a penny. Then he
> called his disciples and said to them, "Truly I tell you, this
> poor widow has put in more than all those who are con-
> tributing to the treasury. For all of them have contributed
> out of their abundance; but she out of her poverty has put
> in everything she had, all she had to live on."*[2]

1. "Mr. Smith Goes to Washington." Directed by Frank Capra, 1939.
2. Mark 12:41–44 and Luke 21:1–4.

41

This is not a parable. The story appears in Mark, our earliest gospel, and also in Luke. It's an observation from everyday life. But I decided to include it with the parables because it is so widely misinterpreted, and I hope to clear that up. The Jesus Seminar were skeptical about whether this was the genuine voice of Jesus and rated the incident gray ("Well, maybe") because similar stories were attributed to other people in antiquity. But it is worth exploring.

The story takes place during Jesus' last week of life. He was in Jerusalem and was peoplewatching outside the Temple treasury where donations were given to support the Temple and the religious establishment. A widow came up to the collection box to give her offering.

## THE WIDOW

We are already familiar with the widow. We met her in chapter two. She is often a powerless person in first-century Jewish society, no longer having a male protector in a patriarchal system. The Torah regularly states that three groups of people fall under God's special care—widows, orphans, and resident aliens—because they have no male or clan protectors. The widow was probably married once but unlikely to wed again. With the mortality rate as high as it was, she could have been in her mid-20s or early-30s.

The widow came up and put in her last two copper pennies in the offering. They were actually "leptons," the smallest Jewish coin worth 1/64 of a silver denarius, which was a daily wage for a twelve-hour day—although a poverty wage at best. In terms of today's comparable wages, a lepton was worth about $1.50. So, two leptons were worth about $3.00. Not a penny, but still comparatively small.

The widow, out of her poverty, gave her all. She would have absolutely nothing to fall back on. She would be completely at the mercy of a world whose cultural norms were set against her. She gave her last two leptons anyway. It was a death sentence. It was all she had to live on. Her last three dollars.

She probably died of hunger mere days after she dropped those two coins into the Temple treasury. Maybe the same day that Jesus was crucified. In case her death shocks or surprises you, consider again what Jesus said about her as she left the Temple that day: "She out of her poverty has put in everything she had—*all she had to live on.*"

## POOR AND HUNGRY PEOPLE

There are an awful lot of poor and hungry people on the planet who survive on little to nothing. Globally, almost 700 million people around the world live on less than $2.15 per day, the World Bank's international line for extreme poverty. Nearly 4 billion people—half of the world's population of 8 billion—live on less than $6.85 a day. The poorest in the world are often undernourished, without access to basic shelter, electricity, and safe drinking water. They have little access to education and suffer from much poorer health.

Children are more than twice as likely as adults to live and die in poverty. Over 333 million children live in extreme poverty. Another 829 million children live below $3.65 in lower–middle income poverty. And 1.43 billion children live below $6.85 in upper–middle income poverty.

Around the world, 50 million people are on the brink of starvation in 45 countries. As many as 19,700 people are estimated to die of hunger every day. This translates to one person dying of hunger every four seconds.

## A "GENEROUS" WIDOW

It may appear that Jesus is glorifying the selfless giving of this poor widow in order to shame the rich into giving more. If that's really what this story is about, then the widow becomes nothing more than an object lesson in what's called "proportional giving." But the widow is not meant to be an object lesson for our stewardship sermons.

This story occurs within Jesus' "Jerusalem ministry," in which he has been confronting the abuses of the Temple system and the corruption of the religious leaders who wield power there. Jesus isn't really speaking about the widow, but of the vicious system which condemns her. He isn't simply saying "good for you!" to this woman and "do like she does!" to his followers, but "you brood of vipers!" to the authorities.

He doesn't say anything about her except that she gave all she had. He doesn't say why, or with what attitude, or whether she should have given away her last two coins or shouldn't have. Jesus meant to show that this widow was entrapped by an abusive Temple and state system that exploited the poorest of the poor. Something is wrong with the system when it takes the last two coins out of a widow's hand. This parable is not about giving sacrificially; it is about pocketing the livelihood of poor and vulnerable people.

This specific passage immediately follows Jesus' rebuking of the scribes for—among other things—financially exploiting vulnerable widows, and it immediately precedes his announcement of the destruction of the Temple. Were we more attuned to the flow of narrative and the broad biblical story, we would see how this account fits into the pattern the gospel writer is weaving. We would hear echoes of the Torah's constant concern for widows, as well as the voices of Hebrew prophets like Isaiah and Amos, who condemned the religious establishment for exploiting the vulnerable.

Lutheran pastor and professor at Lexington Theological Seminary, Leah Schade (b. 1971), once said in a sermon:

> *I used to minister to a widow who was taken in by religious leaders who did this very thing. She would watch the televangelists who looked into the camera—right into her living room—and told her that if she gave all she had, God would bless her. So, every time her Social Security check came, she would write out checks to these televangelists and give them all she had. While she lived in a trailer park barely subsisting in her poverty, the well-dressed women and men on the screen took her money and bought their mansions and their fancy cars and their private jets. And*

*in return she received her "blessing": a cheap "certificate"
touting her as a supporter of their so-called ministry.*[3]

So, is the widow's mite a story about boundless generosity and
self-sacrifice—or is it a tragic tale about Jesus' judgment against religious authorities and those who prey on widows? Preached once
a year, extracted from its context, this widow is offered as a model
to encourage giving to the church. Yet in its context, it suggests a
very different reading: nothing short of a condemnation of the use
of religion to victimize the poor and the powerless.

3. Schade, "The Widow's Mite?"

# CHAPTER 6

# THE GOOD SAMARITAN

*The Bible tells us to love our neighbors,*
*and also to love our enemies;*
*probably because generally they are the same people.*

—Gilbert K. Chesterton (1874–1936)

Jesus was having a discussion with an expert in the law, who was most probably a Pharisee.

> Just then a lawyer stood up to test Jesus. "Teacher," he said, "what must I do to inherit eternal life?" He said to him, "What is written in the law? What do you read there?" He answered, "You shall love the Lord your God with all your heart, and with all your soul, and with all your strength, and with all your mind; and your neighbor as yourself." And he said to him, "You have given the right answer; do this, and you will live." But wanting to justify himself, he asked Jesus, "And who is my neighbor?"

Jesus responded with a parable.

> A man was going down from Jerusalem to Jericho, and fell into the hands of robbers, who stripped him, beat him,

*and went away, leaving him half dead. Now by chance a priest was going down that road; and when he saw him, he passed by on the other side. So likewise, a Levite, when he came to the place and saw him, passed by on the other side. But a Samaritan while traveling came near him; and when he saw him, he was moved with pity. He went to him and bandaged his wounds, having poured oil and wine on them. Then he put him on his own animal, took him to an inn, and took care of him. The next day he took out two denarii, gave them to the innkeeper, and said, "Take care of him; and when I come back, I will repay you whatever more you spend."*[1]

Again, it is impossible to understand the parables without understanding the context in which they were told. One must have some knowledge of the political, religious, and social dimensions of first-century Palestine in order to adequately understand the meaning of these word and picture stories.

## THE ROAD TO JERICHO

Let's start with the road from Jerusalem to Jericho. The distance between the two towns is about 17 miles. The road runs through the Judean desert and rocky hill country. The road was well known for its robberies. This wilderness was populated by bandits and revolutionary Zealots who lived in caves. They were fueled by two conditions: increasing peasant indebtedness resulting in loss of land, and Roman occupation of the country.

The victim is presumably a Jew. He is attacked, stripped of his clothes, beaten, and left half-dead at the side of the road. But being naked, there is no clear way to identify his class, village, or nationality. To Jesus' listeners the victim is "one of us," in a location and situation we can easily imagine.

It was typical for priests and Levites to be walking or riding on this road after performing their weekly duties in the Jerusalem Temple. Many lived in the countryside around Jericho.

1. Luke 10:30–35.

## THE PRIESTLY ARISTOCRACY

The Jewish priesthood was hereditary. Priests traced their lineage to Aaron, the brother of Moses. At the top of the priesthood hierarchy were the high priest and the chief priests. They were the chief administrators of the Temple operations and its treasury.

In the time of Jesus, Judea was ruled by a Roman procurator and not a Jewish king. The high priest was thus the primary representative of the nobility and the most eminent member of the nation. The high priest and 70 chief priests formed the Sanhedrin, the Temple's executive committee and the nation's highest judiciary body. These priests were wealthy members of aristocratic families who lived in Jerusalem. (Note: the lay nobility was referred to as the "elders." Thus the "chief priests and the elders" is a term for the ruling aristocracy.)

Most of these wealthy people were members of the conservative Sadducee party. They represented the religious structure of their day organized around the Temple in Jerusalem. But they also represented the political and legal structure like our executive and judicial branches of government.

## PRIESTS AND LEVITES

Below the priestly aristocracy was a large group of "ordinary" priests. Seven thousand two hundred priests lived throughout the countryside. They were divided into 24 "courses" and served twice a year for a week at the Temple (like Zechariah in Luke 1:5). They also served during the three major religious festivals (Passover, Pentecost, and Tabernacles) when pilgrims were expected to come to Jerusalem. As a result, the priests traveled to Jerusalem at least five times a year to participate in Temple rituals. In the first century, a wide gulf was growing between these lower-class priests and the noble ones in Jerusalem.

Below the priests were the 10,000 Levites. They were members of the tribe of Levi, which was chosen to assist the priests in the Temple. They too lived in the countryside and went to Jerusalem when their weekly shift was on duty. They served as singers and musicians, gatekeepers, sanitation workers, and Temple police officers.

Together, the priests and Levites provided the expertise and the work force to operate the Temple.

## SAMARITANS

Samaria was the region sandwiched between Judea and Galilee. The Samaritans were descended from the northern ten tribes of Israel that had split off from the rest of the nation following King Solomon's reign nine centuries earlier, creating two nations—Israel to the north and Judea to the south. The northern tribes of Israel were eventually conquered by the Assyrians in 722 BCE and large numbers were taken away and resettled in other countries. The people who remained behind in Palestine eventually intermarried with the gentiles who lived in the area and around 400 BCE their descendants emerged as a distinct group: the Samaritans. They had their own version of the Torah, and they constructed their own temple on Mount Gerizim at a time when there was no temple in Jerusalem. They claimed that their temple was the true place of worship, and their priests had a purer blood line than the Judeans.

The Jews (Judeans) regarded the Samaritans as contemptible and corrupt. Their corruption stemmed from two things—a corrupt faith and a racially impure bloodline. The Jews considered them bastards and felt that they were worse than pagans because they at least knew better.

Thus, Jews did not associate with Samaritans. Any place a Samaritan slept was considered unclean, as well as any food or drink that touched the place. A whole village was declared unclean if a Samaritan woman stayed there.

In John's gospel, Jesus is traveling through Samaria and stops to rest by a well. A Samaritan woman comes to the well to draw water and Jesus asks her for a drink.[2] She replied, "You are a Jew,

2. John 4:1–30.

49

and I am a Samaritan woman. How can you ask me for a drink?" The author then adds parenthetically, "For Jews do not associate with Samaritans" or as another source says, "For Jews do not use dishes that Samaritans have used." One rabbi of the first century said, "One who eats the bread of a Samaritan is like one who eats the food of swine." Years earlier, when Jesus was about twelve years old, a group of Samaritans sneaked into the Jerusalem Temple at night during Passover and, in an act of desecration, scattered human bones over the Temple porch and sanctuary.

The animosity was so strong between the two groups that neither was welcome or safe in the other's territory. Jews who traveled through Samaria to go from Galilee to Judea were often attacked in Samaritan territory. On Jesus' journey to Jerusalem, as he traveled through Samaria, his disciples went ahead into a village to prepare for lodging and meals. The villagers did not welcome them, and the disciples returned to Jesus in anger. James and John asked Jesus, "Lord, do you want us to call down fire from heaven to destroy them?" Jesus rebuked them and they went to another village where people were more tolerant.[3] Centuries of religious, racial, and ethnic hatred lay between these two groups of people.

## THE SOCIAL/RELIGIOUS MAP

That expert in the law who asked, "and who is my neighbor?" probably thought the answer would be another Pharisee or at least a Jew with a pure bloodline who obeyed the commandments. Certainly, he could not possibly be neighborly with someone who was sinful or unclean. He maintained a distinct separation from the unwashed "*am ha'aretz*" (*ahm hah-AHR-etz*) or "the people of the land."

For first-century Pharisees, the command to "Be holy because I, Yahweh your God, am holy"[4] shaped their religious experience. Holiness was taken to mean "separation from everything

3. Luke 9:51–56.
4. Lev 19:2.

unclean." Holiness thus meant the same as purity. The desire for purity created a society structured around a purity system. (More about the Pharisees in the next chapter.)

The Jewish community at the time of Jesus was dominated by the fundamental idea of the maintenance of *racial* purity, based on a system of racial superiority. The entire population was classified by purity of descent. Only Israelites of legitimate ancestry formed the pure Israel. The nation was considered God-given, and its purity was God's will. The promises for the age to come were valid only for the pure seed of Israel. Intermarriage was controlled so that only those of pure ancestry could marry others of pure ancestry. (Does this remind you of racial segregation, apartheid, or white Christian nationalism? It should.)

Respectable society consisted of three groups: the priests, the Levites and the Israelites or racially pure laypeople. To the Jews, the Samaritans were at the bottom of the ladder of the social structure just ahead of the Gentiles. The social purity map was organized like this:

- Priests
- Levites
- Israelites (lay people)
- Gentile converts
- Freed Gentile slaves
- Illegitimate children of priests
- Temple slaves
- Bastards
- Fatherless
- Foundlings
- Eunuchs
- Samaritans
- Gentiles

# TRIADIC STORY STRUCTURE

Traditional stories often deal with threes. We see this in fairy tales such as *Goldilocks and the Three Bears*, and *The Three Billy Goats Gruff*. Contemporary jokes also often deal with threes. The first two characters set the stage and the third character delivers the punchline. (A priest, a minister, and a rabbi walk into a bar . . .). Jewish folk tales in the first century also frequently dealt with three characters confronted with the same situation. The whole plot would swing on the third character's actions. This is known as a "triadic structure." The parable of the good Samaritan follows this arrangement. Once Jesus sets the stage with the victim in the ditch, three characters appear.

The reason why the first two characters pass by the victim is not addressed. The priest and the Levite were obligated to maintain a certain level of ritual purity; contact with death was a source of major contamination. The purity law commanded priests not to touch dead bodies or to bury the dead (except their next of kin). The wounded man was described as "half dead," suggesting that one could not tell if he was dead without coming close enough to incur impurity if he was. They probably passed by out of observance of purity laws. At this point Jesus' audience is probably smiling at the discomfort of any clergy in the crowd.

The buildup of suspense focuses on who the next person coming down the road is going to be. The plot is designed to encourage the expectation that a Jewish layperson will appear in the role of hero and bind up the wounds of the injured man. The listeners are ready to identify with this hero. But who shows up coming down the road? A Samaritan, the mortal enemy of the Jewish nation and religion. The story frustrates the listeners' expectations and comes out the wrong way.

The listeners certainly cannot identify with the Samaritan, so they jump in the ditch with the victim. This is not much better. Not only does the story make a hero out of an enemy, but Jesus goes on at length about the generous and kind nature of his compassionate service. Jesus really rubs it in. Accepting compassionate service from an enemy is impossible to comprehend or accept. His listeners become infuriated.

## AN UPSIDE-DOWN KINGDOM

Donald Kraybill (b. 1945), in his book called *The Upside-Down Kingdom*, proposed the thesis that the kingdom of God is an inverted or upside-down way of life in contrast to the prevailing social order. In this parable, the clergy failed the test and the heretic passed. Two "good" people behave evilly, and a "bad" person behaved virtuously. Jesus reverses the social map. He turns it upside-down. This parable again reinforces the idea that in the kingdom of God "many who are first will be last, and the last will be first."[5]

It is interesting to note that nowhere in the parable is the Samaritan called "good." The "good Samaritan" is a term not found in the Bible except for section headings which were not found in the original texts. When a certain ruler addressed Jesus as "good teacher," Jesus said to him, "Why do you call me good? No one is good but God alone."[6] He definitely had strong feelings about labeling people as good or evil.

> *But I say to you, love your enemies and pray for those who persecute you, so that you may be children of your Father in heaven; for he makes his sun rise on the evil and on the good, and sends rain on the righteous and on the unrighteous.*[7]

When the Samaritan reached out to the victim, he stepped across a major social and religious boundary. The message that is being communicated in this parable is that the kingdom of God knows no social, political, or religious boundaries. The great insight of the earliest followers of Jesus was that in the kingdom of God a new kind of social world has come into view. As Paul stated it, "There is no longer any distinction between Jew and Gentile,

---

5. Mark 10:31.

6. Luke 18:19.

7. Matt 5:44–45.

slave or free, male or female."[8] In the kingdom revealed by Jesus, there are no categories for people and no barriers between people. And the ones we do not like, may come ahead of us.

In this parable, our unquestioned assumptions about evil are profoundly undermined. We are forced to acknowledge the goodness of those we detest or distrust—perhaps even accept compassionate service from them. Our supposed enemy may turn out to be our greatest benefactor. The message of the Samaritan may be that the person or event that appears to us to be unmitigated evil is the master disguise in which our neighbor enters our lives in the fullest possible manner.

## ALTERNATIVE PATHS TO BEING RELIGIOUS

There are two ways of being religious. One way involves proper beliefs, religious practices, rituals, laws, and commandments. In this parable, that way is represented by the priest and the Levite. The other way, proposed by Jesus and the prophets, involves compassionate service to other people, including our enemies. The first way involves *religious rules and a fixed morality*; the second way involves *love and compassion.*

According to this parable the kingdom of God has no fixed social, ethnic, racial, nationalistic, economic, or religious boundaries. There are no insiders or outsiders, no elites or nonelites, no good or evil people. For Jesus, compassion was a social paradigm, the core value for life in community. Compassion is a defining characteristic of the conspiracy of love. This is a parable that confronts and confounds the status quo of cultural dividing-lines based on ethnic and racial hierarchies

8. Gal 3:28.

# CHAPTER 7

# THE PHARISEE
# AND THE TAX COLLECTOR

*All paradises, all utopias are designed by who is not there,
by the people who are not allowed in.*

—Toni Morrison (1931–2019)

Jesus told his followers a parable:

> *Two people went up to the temple to pray, one a Pharisee
> and the other a tax collector. The Pharisee, standing by
> himself, was praying thus, 'God, I thank you that I am not
> like other people: thieves, rogues, adulterers, or even like
> this tax collector. I fast once a week; I give a tenth of all my
> income.' But the tax collector, standing far off, would not
> even look up to heaven, but was beating his breast and say-
> ing, 'God, be merciful to me, a sinner!' I tell you; this man
> went down to his home justified rather than the other."*[1]

1. Luke 18:10–14a

## TAX COLLECTORS

In the Roman system, the tax collector or "tax farmer" was a central element for gathering taxes in countries under indirect rule. Local leading citizens were given complete charge of taxation. They raised a crop of taxes for Rome. They bid for their job, based on the amount of taxes they thought they could collect. Any additional money was theirs to keep. These tax collectors were often wealthy at other's expense. They were also thought to be traitors because they collaborated with Roman power in order to gain wealth. Taxes were not used for the common good; they were instead used to support the lifestyles of the rich elites and the ever-hungry power of Rome. We might consider them tributes rather than taxes.

In addition to these direct taxes there were indirect taxes or tolls that were collected on various goods. The collectors of these taxes are called *toll collectors* or *publicans*. They stood at the city gates, in booths along major roads, in major fishing villages, and at other toll collection sites. They were empowered by the chief tax collectors to determine the amount of toll a person had to pay. Publicans were thought to be deceivers and thieves because their profession gave them the right to declare how much toll had to be paid, and of course the right to include some commission for themselves. Many of them were no doubt dishonest. They were therefore considered as vile as robbers and murderers. Tax collectors were so disreputable that in the gospels their title is almost synonymous with "wicked." The phrase "tax collectors and sinners" is a constant pairing.

We are introduced to some of these toll collectors in the gospels. In Mark we meet Levi the toll collector at Capernaum.[2] And in Luke we hear about Zacchaeus the head toll collector at Jericho.[3] When, in Luke, a group of tax collectors approached John the Baptist and asked him what they must do to be saved, he told them not to collect more money than the amount prescribed or appointed.[4]

2. Mark 2:13–17.
3. Luke 19:1–10.
4. Luke 3:10–14.

## SINNERS

Krister Stendahl (1921–2008), former dean of the Harvard Divinity School, used to say that most Christians confess that they are sinners, but really think of themselves as "honorary sinners." In Luke's gospel we are talking about something different. Some translations put the word *sinners* in quotes. It was not meant to refer to sinful individuals as such, but more broadly to a welldefined social class that included most of the poor. The "sinners" were social outcasts.

It included people with immoral occupations like prostitutes, thieves, swindlers, gamblers, usurers, tax collectors, publicans or toll collectors, money changers, and herdsmen, including shepherds. But it also included people with "suspect" occupations, who many people believed were engaged in questionable practices (like Trump lawyers and congressional lobbyists for gun manufacturers today). It also included people with occupations that were considered ritually unclean, like butchers and physicians because they came into contact with blood. People classified as "sinners" could not give testimony in court or hold public office. Consider the shepherds at Jesus birth. Their testimony about the message of the angelic host would have been considered totally untrustworthy.

The sinners would also have included those who did not pay their tithes (one tenth of their income) to the priests, and those who were negligent about the Sabbath rest and about ritual cleanliness. Some scholars believe that the laws and customs on these matters were so complicated that the uneducated poor were quite incapable of understanding what was expected of them. Education in those days was a matter of knowing the scriptures, the law, and all its ramifications. The illiterate and uneducated were inevitably lawless and immoral. The uneducated peasants, "the rabble who know nothing of the law"[5] were regarded by even the most enlightened Pharisees, like Hillel (d. 10 CE), as incapable of virtue and piety.

There was no practical way out for the sinner. Theoretically a prostitute could be made clean again by an elaborate process

5. John 7:49.

of repentance, purification, and atonement. But this would cost money and her illgotten gains could not be used for the purpose. Her money was tainted and unclean. The tax collector would be expected to give up his profession and then make restitution plus onefifth to everyone he had wronged. The likelihood that he could remember everyone and how much he cheated them out of was slim to none. To be a sinner was therefore one's lot. One had been predestined to inferiority by fate or the will of God. In this sense the sinners were captives or prisoners. (Remember that Jesus said he had been called to set the prisoners free.[6])

## PARABOLIC ACTIONS

A key point to remember is that Jesus is criticized for having table fellowship with toll and tax collectors. As Jesus entered Zacchaeus' house, Luke tells us "when they [the crowd] saw it, they all murmured, 'He has gone in to be the guest of a man who is a sinner.'"[7] His actions were incomprehensible for two reasons. First tax collectors were considered unclean because of their profession. Therefore, eating with them would contaminate a good and righteous person. Second, sharing a meal implies acceptance of a person—as they are. A truly righteous person should hold a high standard and refuse to deal with such a sinner unless there is a clear attempt to repent and reform. Instead, Jesus just goes in and parties.

We must realize that not only are Jesus' stories parabolic, but his actions are also. According to the morality of his day, Jesus does things that are clearly wrong and sinful. He and his disciples are viewed as immoral and impure. He challenges the central cultural assumptions of his society by his actions and associations.

> While Jesus was having dinner at Levi's [a tax collector]
> house, many tax collectors and sinners were eating with
> him and his disciples, for there were many who followed
> him. When the teachers of the law who were Pharisees saw

6. Luke 4:18.
7. Luke 19:7–8.

*him eating with the sinners and tax collectors, they asked his disciples: "Why does he eat with tax collectors and sinners?" On hearing this, Jesus said to them, "It is not the healthy who need a doctor, but the sick. I have not come to call the righteous, but sinners."*[8]

## PHARISEES

The Pharisees were a small but powerful movement of lay people who wanted to live holy lives. These were mostly middle-class people: artisans and merchants. Among their membership were rabbis and scribes (people of learning). The Pharisees were often the leaders of the synagogues.

To understand this parable, it is important to try to forget any prejudices you may have about the Pharisees. Modern readers of the New Testament have become accustomed to assume the Pharisees are the "bad guys." Although some Pharisees probably had a holier-than-thou attitude toward others, they enjoyed wide popular support and were highly regarded as good and holy people by others.

In order to live pure and holy lives, the Pharisees thought it was important to isolate themselves from impure things. In Jewish law this included dead bodies, menstruating women, diseased and deformed people, and people with sinful occupations. In order to achieve this isolation, they essentially separated from the rest of society without physically moving away. The name *Pharisee* comes from a word that means "separated."

The Pharisees saw themselves as the faithful remnant of Israel. Their communities were closed associations with restricted membership. You had to be (or seem to be) holy to belong. During a probationary period, you had to prove your ability to follow the ritual laws on purity and tithing. Tithing was very important to the Pharisees.

---

8. Mark 2:15–17.

The Pharisees' view of the kingdom of God was that it would be a kingdom constructed by men through an exact fulfillment of the law and a higher morality. The Pharisees believed that if everyone would fulfill the law perfectly for a single day, the messianic kingdom would come.

Their morality was legalistic, a matter of reward and punishment. They believed that God loved and rewarded those who kept the law and hated and punished those who did not. This led the Pharisees to a belief in an afterlife and the resurrection of the dead for the pious and holy, as compared to the conservative wealthy Sadducees who accepted none of this new-fangled doctrine about life after death. The Sadducees believed the age-old Jewish thought that the mind and soul perished with the body.

## THE HOLINESS MAP

This parable has been generally thought to deal with pride and humility. Luke introduces and concludes this parable in his gospel in such a way as to draw the conclusion that the Pharisee's sin in God's eyes was his pride.

At the Jerusalem Temple, the Pharisee was allowed to enter the court of the Israelites, because of his racial and religious purity. Only priests and Levites could go farther in. The tax collector would have to remain outside the "*hel*," a kind of wall of separation in the Temple complex, because of his impurity in the eyes of his peers.

The Temple as enlarged by Herod was designed in a series of concentric rectangular areas. They represented ten degrees of holiness surrounding the Holy of holies at the Temple's core.[9] People were segregated from the center based on their level of purity. Only the high priest could enter the "holy of holies" and then only on one day a year on Yom Kippur. The Temple map conformed to the purity map of society. Thus, the Temple is a metaphor that stands for insiders and outsiders in first-century Jewish society.

9. Jeremias, *Jerusalem in the Time of Jesus*, 79.

The Temple map consisted of these ten degrees of holiness:

- The holy of holies (the inner sanctuary where God's presence appeared)
- The sanctuary
- The outer area between the porch and the altar
- The court of the priests
- The court of the Israelites (men)
- The court of the women
- The *hel*, a terrace with lattice work, beyond which no Gentile or "sinner" could pass
- The Temple mount[10]
- The city of Jerusalem
- The land of Israel

## PRAYERS

In fact, the Pharisee only did what the Temple *map* required of those who were considered insiders and members of the religious elite of the time. He stands for prayer by himself and says a prayer of thanksgiving. His conduct and prayers are typical of the devout Pharisee.

> *God, I thank you that I am not like other people: thieves, rogues, adulterers, or even like this tax collector. I fast once a week; I give a tenth of all my income.*

10. The Mount refers to a hill called Mount Moriah in the eastern area of Jerusalem. It was the site of Solomon's Temple that was destroyed in 587 BCE. About 50 years later construction of the Second Temple was begun. In around 19 BCE, Herod the Great extended the sacred hilltop's natural plateau by enclosing the area with four massive retaining walls and filling the voids. This artificial expansion resulted in a large flat expanse which today forms the eastern section of the Old City of Jerusalem.

His speech is repeated almost word for word in other examples we have of pious prayers from the same period.

> *Rabbi Judah said: One must utter three phrases every day: Praised be the Lord that He did not make me a heathen, for all heathen are as nothing before Him; praised be He, that He did not make me a woman, for a woman is not under obligation to fulfill the law; praised be He that He did not make me an uneducated man, for the uneducated man is not cautious to avoid sins.*[11]

The same Temple map also determines the place, the stance, and prayer of the tax collector. He belongs to the group who must stay outside the bounds of the Temple in the court of the Gentiles. He stands apart because he knows such is his proper place as an outsider. He would not be allowed to enter further in. Levites serving as guards kept him out. The place that he took was not a demonstration of his humility, as Luke hints, but simply of his awareness of his proper place as a "sinner."

Thus, the two men described in the parable reveal their relative places and status in the accepted culture of the time. One belongs to the sacred precincts of the Temple and is an insider. The other belongs to the secular world and is an outsider. Their positions are symbolic of their culture's view of their closeness to God—one near and one far. Jesus stuns the hearers with his conclusion: "The tax collector went home to his house justified" (meaning acquitted, absolved, vindicated, free from blame, declared "not guilty"). The Pharisee did not.

Luke attributes this statement to the humility of the tax collector and to the pride of the Pharisee, but the tax collector remains a "sinner." He does not make restitution for his extortions as Zacchaeus did.[12] The Pharisee simply thanked God for his good deeds, as was customary in the prayers of a devout Pharisee of his time. Both had their prayers answered. The tax collector asked God to be merciful to him. The Pharisee asked for nothing. His

---

11. Scott, *Hear then the Parable*, 95.
12. Luke 19:1–9.

was an informative prayer. He just told God what, in his opinion, was going on.

## STORIES THAT COME OUT WRONG

If we are right in our theory that parables are stories that come out wrong—that reverse listeners' expectations—then something else is going on here besides pride and humility. It is almost as if the story is saying that closeness to the "holy of holies" does not indicate closeness to God. The map has been reversed. God is no longer in the Temple only available to insiders but is outside in the secular world available to outsiders and outcasts. They may be closer to God than the righteous insiders.

> Jesus said to them [the chief priests and the elders], "Truly I tell you, the tax collectors and the prostitutes are entering the kingdom of God ahead of you."

As we have shown, the Temple is a metaphor for this myth, the central myth of Judaism. It is founded on the words "Be holy because I, Yahweh your God, am holy."[13] Jesus introduces a new image of God—the compassionate one. He proposes a new way of religious expression, "Be compassionate as your Father is compassionate."[14]

When this parable is placed alongside that of the good Samaritan, the main point emerges with stark clarity. The religious map of the time is being abandoned. Those who represent the religious establishment of the day—priests, Levites, and Pharisees—are found wanting, and those who represent immorality and impurity—the Samaritan and the tax collector—are those who are justified and accepted by God.

The kingdom of God is not to be found in the Temple. Nor is it restricted to the church. The activity of the kingdom has moved from the sacred precincts of the Temple to the profane arena of the secular world. The Pharisee represents the piety and purity

13. Lev 19:2.
14. Luke 6:36.

of the Temple. The tax collector represents the sinfulness of the secular world. The sacred place is no longer the place of the sacred. Divinity has moved into the world of everyday life. God no longer dwells in the Holy of Holies, but rather has pitched his tent among people—particularly those who are lost, estranged, and separated from him.

In his parables Jesus abolishes the difference between the holy and the unholy, the sacred and the profane, the religious insider and the outsider. All of life is part of the kingdom of God—including the dirty and the nasty parts.

## THE MYTH OF GOOD AND EVIL

Once again Jesus confronts our ideas of defining and separating good and bad. He states that God is not just concerned about good people. "God causes his sun to rise on the evil and the good and sends rain on the righteous and the unrighteous."[15] God loves and accepts everyone. What is unacceptable to Jesus is that we should decide *on our own* what is good and what is evil. French theologian and lawyer Jacques Ellul (1912–1994) said that only God can decide who or what is good.

> *What God decides, whatever it may be, is the good. If then, we decide what the good is, we substitute our own will for God's. We construct a morality when we say what is good. It is then that we are radically sinners. What Adam and Eve acquired when they took the fruit, is the knowledge of good and evil. That is, they took on the right to state, as God does, that this is good and that is bad." Only God can define good and evil. Our criteria, our decision to judge, is the great sin of mankind.*
> *That is why Jesus attacks the Pharisees so severely even though they are the most moral of people, live the best lives, and are perfectly obedient and virtuous. They have progressively substituted their own morality for the living word of God that can never be fixed in commandments. Jesus gives as his own commandment 'Follow me,' not a list*

15. Matt 5:45.

*of things to do or not to do. He shows us what it means to be a free person with no morality, but simply obeying the ever-new word of God as it flashes forth in our lives. Love, which cannot be regulated, categorized, or analyzed into principles or commandments, takes the place of law. The relationship with others is not one of duty but of love.*[16]

Ellul claims that this is the message of the parables.

*Revelation is an attack on all morality, as is wonderfully shown by the parables of the kingdom of God, that of the prodigal son, that of the talents, that of the eleventh-hour laborers, that of the unfaithful steward, and many others. In all the parables the person who serves as an example has not lived a moral life. The one who is rejected is the one who has lived a moral life. Naturally this does not mean that we are counseled to become robbers, murderers, adulterers, etc. On the contrary, the behavior to which we are summoned surpasses morality, all morality, which is shown to be an obstacle to encounter with God.*[17]

Following Jesus involves breaking down the barriers that divide us, overcoming judgment with acceptance, and replacing morality with compassion.

16. Ellul, *The Subversion of Christianity*, 70.

17. Ellul, *The Subversion of Christianity*, 71.

# CHAPTER 8

# THE PRODIGAL SON

*All roads out of hell lead home.*

—SHANNON ALDER (B. 1970)

JESUS TOLD THE PEOPLE a parable:

*There was a man who had two sons. The younger of them said to his father, "Father give me the share of this property that will belong to me." So, he divided the property between them. A few days later the younger son gathered all he had and traveled to a distant country, and there he squandered his property in dissolute living. When he had spent everything, a severe famine took place throughout that country, and he began to be in need. So, he went and hired himself out to one of the citizens of that country, who sent him to his fields to feed the pigs. He would gladly have filled himself with the pods that the pigs were eating; and no one gave him anything. But when he came to himself, he said, "How many of my father's hired hands have bread enough and to spare, but here I am dying of hunger! I will get up and go to my father, and I will say to him, 'Father, I have sinned against heaven and before you; I am no longer worthy to be called your son, treat me like one of your hired hands.'"*

*So, he set off and went to his father. But while he was still far off, his father saw him and was filled with compassion; he ran and put his arms around him and kissed him. Then the son said to him, "Father, I have sinned against heaven and before you; I no longer worthy to be called your son." But the father said to his slaves, "Quickly, bring out a robe—the best one—and put it on him, put a ring on his finger and sandals on his feet. And get the fatted calf and kill it and let us eat and celebrate; for this son of mine was dead and is alive again; he was lost and is found." And they began to celebrate.*

*Now, his elder son was in the field; and when he came and approached the house, he heard music and dancing. He called one of the slaves and asked what was going on. He replied, "Your brother has come, and your father has killed the fatted calf because he has got him back safe and sound." Then he became angry and refused to go in. His father came out and began to plead with him. But he answered his father, "Listen! For all these years I have been working like a slave for you, and I have never disobeyed your command; yet you have never given me even a young goat so that I might celebrate with my friends. But when this son of yours came back, who has devoured your property with prostitutes, you killed the fatted calf for him!" Then the father said to him, "Son, you are always with me, and all that is mine is yours. But we had to celebrate and rejoice, because this brother of yours was dead and has come to life, he was lost and has been found."[1]*

This parable demonstrates another example of threes in story telling—this story has three episodes or acts. It also uses the rule of *stage duality*, in which no more than two characters share the scene and dialog at any time.

This parable takes place in the context of a society where everyone was assigned a fixed place in the class structure. In that society a father was the representative of the law. The inheritance was of extreme importance and was governed by a legal code and

1. Luke 15:11–32.

maintained by strict rules. The father's role was to protect both the honor of the family and the inheritance. According to Deuteronomy 21:15–17, the eldest son inherits twice as much as the other sons. In this situation, the younger of two sons was entitled to a third of the property. The inheritance could be divided prior to his death, but the property could not be sold until the father's death. It was the duty of the sons to use this property to take care of their father in his old age. (In this exclusively male patriarchal system, daughters could not inherit anything.)

## ACT ONE

The story begins with the younger son who demands his inheritance ahead of schedule and then, having received it, takes off for the good life. We are told he goes to a distant country. In the first century, Jewish people has been dispersed to many lands by many centuries of conquerors. Many never returned to Palestine. Across the Mediterranean region Jews of the Diaspora numbered about four million, compared to about half a million in Palestine.

The story then describes the son's progressive degradation. He squanders his (and his father's) property in dissolute living. He finally winds up in disaster. Famine comes upon the country, and he has nothing to eat. To avoid starving, he takes a job caring for pigs, an occupation that was considered an abandonment of the Jewish religion. Swine were regarded as unclean animals.[2] In short, the prodigal hits bottom from every perspective. (The term "prodigal" means a person who spends money in a recklessly extravagant way.)

Then, the story says, "he came to himself." In Hebrew and Aramaic, this is an expression of repentance. He starts trudging back in his rags and smelling to high heaven from the pigsty. He has jeopardized the family's economic standing and put his father at risk by squandering that part of his inheritance that belonged by right to his father in his old age. Besides flagrant ingratitude,

2. Lev 11:7 and Deut 14:8.

he has added the sin of injustice. No longer entitled to be fed and clothed by his father, he decides to ask to be hired as a worker.


## ACT TWO

His father sees his wayward son coming home in the distance. He is filled with compassion. (That is the same phrase used for the good Samaritan—filled with pity, mercy, compassion.) The father dashes out, runs down the road and covers his son with affectionate embraces and kisses. His free expression of love is totally out of character for a father in a patriarchal society. So is running. It would be considered undignified. Here, then, is a father who disregards his honor, the inheritance, and the accepted patriarchal standards of the time, and acts like a mother.

The kiss, a reference to 2 Samuel 14:33, is a sign of forgiveness, given even before the son makes his confession. When the prodigal acknowledges his sin, the father does not even listen to his carefully prepared speech and the part about his becoming a hired hand. He immediately calls for the best robe, which is probably one of his own. A fine robe is a mark of high distinction. A signet ring is a sign of authority. The sandals are a luxury, worn by free men. Killing the fatted calf is unusual because beef is rarely eaten. This is the mark of a special feast. Rather than a hired hand, the father treats his son as an honored guest. The music and dancing begin.

But the story doesn't end here.


## ACT THREE

The elder son now appears. He has been faithfully serving his father on the land and working diligently for his share of the inheritance. The disappearance of the younger son has put his own share in jeopardy because now he is going to have to provide for his father's old age entirely out of his own resources. He has reason to be indignant at his younger brother and refers to him contemptuously as "that son of yours."

On the other hand, by refusing to go into the party, the elder son sins against the fourth commandment, which requires him to honor his father. When his father graciously comes out to remonstrate with him, the elder son berates the old man for his goodness saying, "You have rewarded this son of yours who has not only wasted his share of the family fortune, but by living with prostitutes has risked the family blood line." Along with his offensive language, he dishonors both his father and his brother by refusing to take part in the celebration. Thus, he has broken the legal code of the time just as much as the younger son, but in his own way.

One thing to note is the similar refrain at the end of acts two and three: "This son of mine (this brother of yours) was dead and is alive again; he was lost and is found."

## THE MYTH OF THE CHOSEN AND THE REJECTED

This parable may be intended to subvert one of the favorite themes of the Hebrew Bible—namely that of the chosen and the rejected. The Hebrew Bible is filled with stories of two sons: Cain and Abel, Ishmael and Isaac, Esau and Jacob, Joseph and Benjamin. Many of these stories follow a stereotype: the younger sons often leave their father's house to seek their fortune, There is something slightly scandalous or off-color in their behavior; and they are their father's favorite.

The expectation is that the elder son in this story is also going to be rejected. That creates some problems for the listener. If they want to identify with the chosen one, they must identify with a sinner, a swineherd, and a wastrel. If they identify with the righteous son, they might risk not being chosen. Instead of rejecting the elder son for his disrespect, the father affirms, "You are always with me. Everything I have is yours." The elder son thus is assured of his inheritance in spite of his misconduct. Just as the younger son is received back into the family in spite of dissipating his father's livelihood, so the elder son, who has just broken the fourth commandment by his insolent disrespect, is restored to favor. The father thus disregards the offenses of *both* sons. He puts completely aside his personal honor and the legal code. He shows himself equally disinterested in the immorality of his younger son and in the offensive self-righteousness that is the pre-occupation of his elder son. Apparently, the requirements of the Mosaic law are of no real importance to him. His conduct upstages both the misconduct of the younger son and the insistence on legal rights of the elder.

The parable must have left the Jewish audience with their mouths open in astonishment. What they thought was their major claim to God's protection and love, his designation of them as his chosen people, is profoundly undermined by this parable. The fact is that *everyone* is chosen. This includes both public sinners and the self-righteous who deny their complicity in sin.

The father of this parable does not punish sin, nor does he reward righteous behavior. Spiritual brownie points do not count. According to Jesus, his heavenly father is not particularly interested in legal codes and in conventional morality. He seeks the unity of the human family, the removal of divisions and barriers, and the triumph of compassion. It is to unite his two sons: to bring them together in love. Both are guilty of serious failings, and he wants to forgive them both. This father's concern is not justice, but compassion and mercy. The father communicates unconditional love to his two sons so that they in turn may show compassion to each other. This father forgives them both and fervently wants them to live together in peace and common concern. He wants their reconciliation. He has forgiven his youngest son, now he wants the elder son to do the same.

# CHAPTER 9

# THE RICH FOOLS

*A rich man is nothing but a poor man with money.*
—W. C. FIELDS (1880–1946)

IN 2024, THE UNITED States ranked first with the most billionaires (813) worth a collective $5.7 trillion. Altogether, the planet's billionaires are now worth $14.2 trillion. Elon Musk fell from first place to second after his pricey acquisition of Twitter (now renamed X) helped sink Tesla shares. Bernard Arnault, head of luxury goods giant LVMH—including Tiffany, Christian Dior, Louis Vuitton, Givenchy, Bulgari, and Sephora—took his place as the world's richest person, marking the first time a citizen of France led the ranking. Further down the list are the familiar names of Jeff Bezos, Mark Zuckerberg, Warren Buffet, Bill Gates, and hundreds of others.

During the past two years, $26 trillion (63 percent) of all new wealth was captured by the globe's richest one percent, while $16 trillion (37 percent) went to the rest of the world put together. This comes on top of a decade of historic gains—the number and wealth of billionaires having doubled over the last ten years. The World Bank says we are likely seeing the biggest increase in global inequality and poverty since the Second World War. According to Gabriela Bucher (b. 1973), Executive Director of Oxfam International:

> While ordinary people are making daily sacrifices on essentials like food, the super-rich have outdone even their wildest dreams. Just two years in, this decade is shaping up to be the best yet for billionaires—a roaring '20s boom for the world's richest.

Jesus told a parable about rich people accumulating more and more wealth for themselves. This is the only parable where God becomes an actual character in the story.

> And [Jesus] said to them, 'Take care! Be on your guard against all kinds of greed; for one's life does not consist in the abundance of possessions.'
> Then he told them a parable: 'The land of a rich man produced abundantly. And he thought to himself, "What should I do, for I have no place to store my crops?" Then he said, "I will do this: I will pull down my barns and build larger ones, and there I will store all my grain and my goods. And I will say to myself, 'Self, you have ample goods laid up for many years; relax, eat, drink, be merry.'" But God said to him, "You fool! This very night your life is being demanded of you. And the things you have prepared, whose will they be?"
> So, it is with those who store up treasures for themselves but are not rich towards God.'[1]

The kingdom of God was surely the most common subject of Jesus' teaching, but the second was the danger of wealth.

## COTTON PATCH VERSION

Clarence Jordan (1912–1969) offers a unique perspective on this parable. Jordan was an American farmer and the founder of Koinonia Farm, a small but influential integrated religious community in the segregated Georgia of the 1940s. He was also New Testament

1. Luke 12:15–21.

Greek scholar and the author of the *Cotton Patch* translation of the New Testament which set the stories in the location and dialect of Georgia.

The *Cotton Patch* translation of the introduction of the parable brings out its original earthiness: "You all be careful and stay on your guard against all kinds of greediness. For a person's life is not for the piling up of possessions." Jordan then develops this parable in an interesting way in *The Substance of Faith and Other Cotton Patch Sermons*. He elevates the parable to a broad social and political level.

> Jesus said, "There was a certain rich farmer." Now, he didn't say what the man's name was. Jesus left him rather impersonal. To make it a little bit more personal, let's give the man a name. We'll call him Sam. "Sam's fields brought forth abundantly." Now, we might even want to call him uncle. That would be all right, too. "Uncle Sam's fields brought forth abundantly."[2]

And what did Uncle Sam do with his rich yield? He kept it all to himself and ignored the hungry people around him. So, although the parable may have been intended to be understood on a purely individual basis, we could legitimately expand the reading to include the nation and the entire world and thereby invite a new lesson. In either reading, the problem is greediness and self-interest, an unwillingness to share with those in need. The times and circumstances of U.S. politics have waxed and waned over the years since Clarence Jordan wrote in 1972, but today there is one political party standing for the greed of the wealthiest Americans and against a social safety net for the most vulnerable. (Hint: It's the Republican party.)

Filling storehouses with grain in years of plenty, to guard against lean years is familiar to the ears of Jesus' listeners.[3] But they expect it to benefit the wider community. The rich man makes it clear that he alone is the beneficiary. And he intends to build

---

2. Jordan, *Substance of Faith,* 81–82.

3. Gen 41:46–57.

even larger storehouses rather than share his wealth with anyone else, especially the poor.

The interesting thing, and maybe the key point, is revealed when God says to the rich farmer, "You fool! This very night your life is being demanded of you" (NRSV). Many other translators have a similar reading of the Greek text: "Fool! This night your soul is required of you" (ESV); "You fool! You will die this very night" (NLT); "You fool! This very night your life will be demanded back from you" (NET). But those translations miss the real meaning of the Greek text. In a newer translation, *The New Testament* by David Bentley Hart (b. 1965), we find a more literal translation: "Fool, this night they demand your soul from you."

Clarence Jordan explains it this way:

> God didn't kill that man. It's the third person plural. "They
> are demanding your soul from you." Who is "they"? All
> these barns, all these granaries, all these fields, all this stuff
> he has given himself over the years. They are demanding.[4]

It is not that the rich farmer will die, but that his wealth and his possessions are demanding control of his life—lock, stock, and barrel. He now lives in bondage to the very things he thought would serve him.

Jesus was not an ascetic. He did not fast like John the Baptizer and his disciples. We are told that he loved to feast with others and enjoyed the abundance of a shared meal. Jesus loved to eat, drink, and be merry. He did not condemn the farmer for enjoying life. But at the same time, Jesus often rebuked those who set their eyes on possessions, because the accumulation of possessions often separates us from other people. Our focus turns inward. The danger is that we may become self-serving, self-centered, and selfish. Jesus said we cannot serve two masters: "You cannot serve both God and money."[5] When wealth and possessions demand our souls, they become our masters, and we become their servants.

4. Jordan, *Cotton Patch Sermons*, 82.
5. Luke 16:13.

## THE RICH MAN AND LAZARUS

In another parable, that of the rich man and Lazarus, Jesus reportedly described a different rich man who had great possessions and lived in a large mansion in a gated community and feasted sumptuously.

This parable is in dispute as to whether it genuinely goes back to Jesus. Especially the last part which says, "If someone goes to them [the rich man's five brothers] from the dead, they will repent." He [Abraham] said to him, "If they do not listen to Moses and the prophets, neither will they be convinced even if someone rises from the dead." This sounds like an addition by a later Christian community wanting to tie in the resurrection. But despite the questionable authenticity, the parable makes a legitimate point.

Outside of the rich man's gate lay a poor man, hoping for scraps from the rich man's table. In his absolute distress, he may have been placed by the rich man's gate by others in hope that the rich man, his family, or his guests would notice the poor sick man and have pity on his condition. The Hebrew law commanded an appropriate response:

> Since there will never cease to be some needy on the earth,
> I [Yahweh] therefore command you, "Open your hand to
> the poor and needy neighbor in your land."[6]

The book of Tobit, included in Roman Catholic and Eastern Orthodox bibles, also comments:

> Give alms from your possessions, and do not let your eye
> begrudge the gift when you make it. Do not turn your face
> away from anyone who is poor, and the face of God will
> not be turned away from you . . . for almsgiving delivers
> from death and keeps you from going into the darkness.[7]

Although we don't know the rich man's name, the poor man was named Lazarus. He and Abraham are the only two individuals, aside from God, named in Jesus' parables, and both are found

6. Deut 15:11.
7. Tob 4:7–10.

in this one. In Hebrew, Lazarus would have been Eliezer, which means "God [El] helps." But as we know from observation and experience, God does not help the poor without a human actor. In this case the potential actor refused to act on God's behalf.

The rich man ignored the poor man's plight and the poor man soon died from hunger and disease. Not long after, the rich man also died. In Sheol, the shadowy land of the dead under the ground, the rich man and the poor man experienced a reversal of fortune.

> There was a rich man who was dressed in purple and fine linen and who feasted sumptuously every day. And at his gate lay a poor man named Lazarus, covered with sores, who longed to satisfy his hunger with what fell from the rich man's table; even the dogs would come and lick his sores. The poor man died and was carried away by the angels to be with Abraham. The rich man also died and was buried. In Sheol, where he was being tormented, he looked up and saw Abraham far away with Lazarus by his side. He called out, "Father Abraham, have mercy on me, and send Lazarus to dip the tip of his finger in water and cool my tongue; for I am in agony in these flames." But Abraham said, "Child, remember that during your lifetime you received your good things, and Lazarus in like manner evil things; but now he is comforted here, and you are in agony. Besides all this, between you and us a great chasm has been fixed, so that those who might want to pass from here to you cannot do so, and no one can cross from there to us."
>
> He said, "Then, father, I beg you to send him to my father's house—for I have five brothers—that he may warn them, so that they will not also come into this place of torment." Abraham replied, "They have Moses and the prophets; they should listen to them." He said, "No, Father Abraham; but if someone goes to them from the dead, they will repent." He said to him, "If they do not listen to Moses and the prophets, neither will they be convinced even if someone rises from the dead."[8]

8. Luke 16:19–31.

This rich man is not condemned for being wealthy; he is guilty of being indifferent to his poor neighbors, to the beggars at his gate. Elie Wiesel (1928–2016) once said, "The opposite of love is not hate, it's indifference." The rich man simply did not love his neighbors. He was uncaring and unloving. He developed a heart of stone.

This parable is not about heaven and hell. It presents an ancient belief that after death there is a continued existence in a shadowy underworld with a chasm dividing a place of suffering from a place of comfort. For the Hebrews it was Sheol, for the Greeks it was Hades. In Greek mythology Hades is the god of the dead and the king of the underworld, with which his name became synonymous. Hades along with his brothers Zeus and Poseidon claimed joint rulership over the cosmos. Hades received the underworld, Zeus the sky, and Poseidon the sea, with the solid earth available to all three concurrently. In Greek mythology all people went to Hades after death. The Asphodel Meadows is the location in the underworld where the majority of the deceased dwell. According to Plato, souls were judged after death and the wicked were sent to Tartarus, a deep abyss that is used as a dungeon of torment and suffering. The wicked were judged on the basis of how they lived, not what they believed or disbelieved. We can see the parallels of the Greek scheme in the Hebrew Sheol.

## SINFULNESS AS SELFISHNESS

For centuries, Christian theologians have defined sin as missing a target of ideal human behavior, or violating select divine commandments, or even being in a state of rebellion against or separation from God. Today, others define sin as the fundamental state of ego-centrism that consumes our lives. At its core, sin in both the individual and the social context is rooted in human self-centeredness, self-obsession, and selfishness. It is found in the condition of living for oneself alone and a callous disregard for the needs of others. My desk dictionary lists 142 compound words that begin with the word *self*, including self-absorption, self-concern, self-centeredness, self-importance, self-indulgence, self-interest, self-righteousness, self-serving, and selfishness. This is the underlying nature of human sin—an overwhelmingly dominant focus on myself, my needs, and my desires.

As humans our hearts are filled with worry, insecurity, and self-concern. We are anxious about the future. Whether we admit it or not, we perceive the world as a cruel place, and realize that in a largely selfish world, others will surely be indifferent to our needs and welfare. We thus believe we must care for ourselves first and provide for our own future security at the expense of anyone else. The egotistic self thus pursues goals that attempt to insulate and protect it from a seemingly random and harmful universe. We search for a sense of security through wealth, possessions, pleasure, prestige, power, exclusive solidarity, and self-centered religion. In the process, our hearts become concentrated in our materialistic culture and the things that conventional wisdom deems to be of importance.

This focus on the self often leads to alienation, isolation, and separation from others. A life lived for oneself results in a hard and cold heart. It drives out compassion and concern for the needs of others. It often spawns a desire to dominate and control others in service to the self. Selfishness is at the root of those enduring political systems in which a few wealthy and powerful people control the economic life of the many, extracting their productivity to maintain luxurious lifestyles.

## THE DOMINATION SYSTEM

Throughout history, nearly every society has favored an elite group of individuals and families at the expense of the majority of less-fortunate inhabitants. For thousands of years, economic elites have rigged society in their favor by crafting systems that would benefit their prosperity and ensure their control over the nation's political and economic affairs. Historically, they have used unjust economic systems to extract wealth from the sweat of slaves, peasants, and laborers, while contributing little to the common welfare. Social control has been maintained with violence and military might, often supported by religious institutions. These societies have invariably been patriarchies where the authority and desires of men have dominated the lives of women and children. The system has frequently favored one race, tribe, or ethnic group over others.

Biblical scholar Walter Wink (1935–2012) has referred to these societies as manifestations of an enduring *domination system* that has been part of the human story since the rise of civilization in the ancient near east. Wink describes the domination system in this way:

> *It is characterized by unjust economic relations, oppressive political relations, biased race relations, patriarchal gender relations, hierarchical power relations, and the use of violence to maintain them all. No matter what shape the dominating system of the moment might take (from the ancient Near Eastern states to the Pax Romana to feudal Europe to communist state capitalism to modern market capitalism), the basic structure has persisted now for at least five thousand years, since the rise of the great conquest states of Mesopotamia around 3000 BCE.*[9]

In the market system of capitalism, individuals pursue their exclusive self-interest. That is the basis of capitalist economic theory, but it has always posed a moral problem in relation to the contrasting idea of the common good held by many religions. Capitalist philosophers claim that when the self-interest of capitalists is pursued without restraint, everyone benefits—but that has rarely been the case. Economist John Kenneth Galbraith (1908–2006) once commented:

> *The modern conservative is engaged in one of man's oldest exercises in moral philosophy; that is, the search for a superior moral justification for selfishness.*[10]

---

9. Wink, *The Powers That Be*, 39–40.

10. Galbraith, "Let us Begin," *Harpers*.

## SHARED WEALTH

Uncle Sam's fields have brought forth abundantly, but the abundance has not been shared with the working poor and their children, nor with those in need of healthcare, nor with the elderly in Medicaid-funded nursing homes. Massive tax cuts for the wealthiest, bloated military budgets, welfare for giant corporations, vast prison systems, and cuts to social services for the poorest Americans are all signs of the present manifestation of Uncle Sam's domination system. The top one percent build bigger barns on the Cayman Islands to store their wealth, while ignoring the needs of the many who suffer.

Walter Wink notes that the teachings of Jesus were a prescriptive remedy to the domination system of his time. The kingdom of God that Jesus pictured in his parables is an antidote to the status quo. The vision of Jesus stands in direct opposition to the political and economic aims of these pervasively unjust social structures. It is a vision of the domination system turned upside-down. Therefore, every act of resistance to the domination system, every protest of its unjust laws and structures, every effort to transform it for the common good is a sign of the kingdom of God that Jesus proclaimed.

In the conspiracy of love, all typical domination values are reversed. The first shall be last and the last shall be first. The greatest people in the kingdom shall be servants. The powerful shall be brought low and the lowly lifted up—not in a heavenly existence but here on earth. The hungry shall be filled with good things and the rich sent away empty. The kingdom of God particularly belongs to the poor, the hungry, the mourning, and the marginalized because they will gladly welcome its coming. The rich will find it almost impossible to enter the kingdom community because they are too entrenched in the way things are and will resist the change it promises.

We cannot eliminate the dark side of the human condition, but we can summon the better angels of our nature to make us a more humane, kind, and decent people. Even if persistent social selfishness cannot be eliminated, it can be mitigated and minimized by people of good will. The hope of the conspiracy of love is that a transformation of the politics of selfishness is possible through the efforts of transformed individuals who are committed to nonviolent social change motivated by love and compassion.

# CHAPTER 10

# THE DINNER PARTY

*The table is a meeting place, a gathering ground,*
*the source of sustenance and nourishment,*
*festivity, safety, and satisfaction.*
*A person cooking is a person giving:*
*even the simplest food is a gift.*

—LAURIE COLWIN (1944–1992)

A DINNER PARTY IS an act of communion. Someone is inviting you to sit down with them. It's a gesture of generosity, of peacemaking, of intimacy, of trust. On one occasion when Jesus was going to the house of a leader of the Pharisees to eat a meal on the sabbath, he said to the one who had invited him:

> *When you give a luncheon or a dinner, do not invite your friends or your brothers or your relatives or rich neighbors, in case they may invite you in return, and you would be repaid. But when you give a banquet, invite the poor [ptóchos], the crippled, the lame, and the blind. And you will be blessed because they cannot repay you.*[1]

---

1. Luke 14:12–13.

Then he told this parable:

> *Someone gave a great dinner and invited many. At the time for the dinner, he sent his slave to say to those who had been invited, "Come; for everything is ready now." But they all alike began to make excuses. The first said to him, "I have bought a piece of land, and I must go out and see it; please accept my apologies." Another said, "I have bought five yoke of oxen, and I am going to try them out; please accept my apologies." Another said, "I have just been married, and therefore I cannot come." So, the slave returned and reported this to his master. Then the owner of the house became angry and said to his slave, "Go out at once into the streets and lanes of the town and bring in the poor [ptóchos], the crippled, the blind, and the lame." And the slave said, "Sir, what you ordered has been done, and there is still room." Then the master said to the slave, "Go out into the roads and lanes, and compel people to come in, so that my house may be filled. For I tell you, none of those who were invited will taste my dinner."*[2]

This parable from Luke is also found in the gospel of Thomas, although the details differ. There is another parable in Matthew's gospel, that of the wedding banquet (Matthew 22), although that parable is clearly an allegory, its authenticity is suspect, and was unlikely to have been told by Jesus.

## THOMAS

The gospel of Thomas is a sayings gospel; it has no narrative life of Jesus. It was discovered near Nag Hammadi, Egypt, in December 1945 among a group of books known as the Nag Hammadi library. It is composed of 114 sayings attributed to Jesus. Almost two-thirds of these sayings resemble those found in the canonical gospels. Scholars speculate that the works were hidden in response to a letter from Bishop Athanasius of Alexandria (d. 373) declaring a strict canon of Christian scripture. It is suggested that, in his

2. Luke 14:16–24.

Easter letter of 367, Athanasius was the first person to list the 27 books of the New Testament canon that are in use today. The list did not include the gospel of Thomas.

The parable of the banquet in Thomas goes like this:

> Jesus said, "A man was receiving out-of-town visitors. And having prepared the dinner, he sent a slave to invite the visitors. The slave went first and said to that one, 'My master invites you.' That person said, 'Some wholesale merchants owe me money; they are coming to me this evening, and I shall go and give them instructions. I must decline the dinner invitation.' The slave went to another and said to that one, 'My master invites you.' That person said to the slave, 'I have bought a building, and I am needed for a time. I am not free.' The slave went to another and said to that one, 'My master invites you.' That person said to the slave, 'My friend is about to get married, and it is I who am going to give the dinner. I cannot come; I must decline the dinner invitation.' The slave went to another and said to that one, 'My master invites you.' That person said to the slave, 'I have bought a village; I am going to collect the rents. I cannot come, I must decline.' The slave came and said to its master, 'The people you have invited to the dinner have declined.' The master said to his slave, 'Go outside into the streets; bring in whomever you find, to have dinner.'"[3]

As you can see, the two parables in Luke and Thomas are quite similar. In both, the dinner party is a metaphor for the kingdom of God. It is a celebratory meal for many different kinds of people, especially the poor, crippled, disabled, and blind who are found begging for food along the road. They welcome the invitation and gladly accept. The rich have already turned it down.

## EXCUSES AND SHAME

In Luke's parable, Jesus summarizes the actions of the original invitees: "they all alike began to make excuses." In this parable, the people who decline the invitation are those who bought land,

3. Thom 64.

bought five oxen, or recently got married. In Thomas' parable, they are those who are owed money and must collect, have bought a building, must plan a wedding banquet for a friend, or have bought an entire village and must collect rents. They are clearly all elites; no poor person could do any of this. And they all have rejected an invitation to be part of the kingdom of God because they are too busy. It's not a priority.

The man who invited the guests is dishonored by their actions. Honor and shame were very important in Near Eastern society. By inviting those in the roads, lanes, or streets, the man who gave the banquet subverts the system of honor and welcomes the shameless poor.

The poor will gladly welcome the kingdom of God. They are promised food and drink, celebration and levity. After all, theirs is the kingdom according to Jesus.

> *Looking at his disciples, he said: "Blessed are you who are poor [ptóchos], for yours is the kingdom of God. Blessed are you who hunger now, for you will be satisfied. Blessed are you who weep now, for you will laugh.*[4]

But the wealthy will not welcome the kingdom. They are too concerned with their own affairs. If the banquet represents an intrusion on the status quo, they don't want any part of it. And they are unlikely to want to mix with the poor, the crippled, the blind, the lame, and all manner of "sinners."

---

4. Luke 6:20–21.

# CHAPTER 11

# THE LAST JUDGEMENT

*Every day is Judgement Day.*
*Always has been. Always will be.*

—Tom Robbins (b. 1932)

The tale of the final judgment for all of humanity is found in Matthew 25. Matthew weaves it into a story about reward and punishment. This is not generally considered a parable. To be a genuine parable it would reverse our expectations of rewards and punishments and the ability to designate good and bad people. The Jesus Seminar designated it as "black" as in "There's been some mistake. This is not Jesus." In spite of that, there is some of Jesus that comes through if you can get past Matthew's writing—a kernel of truth towards the kind of behavior that Jesus wants and expects from us.

According to Matthew, Jesus told his followers a story:

> *When the Son of Man comes in his glory, and all the angels*
> *with him, then he will sit on the throne of his glory. All the*
> *nations will be gathered before him, and he will separate*
> *people one from another as a shepherd separates the sheep*

*from the goats, and he will put the sheep at his right hand
and the goats at the left.*

*Then the king will say to those at his right hand,
"Come, you that are blessed by my Father, inherit the kingdom prepared for you from the foundation of the world;
for I was hungry and you gave me food, I was thirsty and
you gave me something to drink, I was a stranger and you
welcomed me, I was naked and you gave me clothing, I
was sick and you took care of me, I was in prison and you
visited me." Then the righteous will answer him, "Lord,
when was it that we saw you hungry and gave you food, or
thirsty and gave you something to drink? And when was it
that we saw you a stranger and welcomed you, or naked
and gave you clothing? And when was it that we saw you
sick or in prison and visited you?" And the king will answer
them, "Truly I tell you, just as you did it to one of the least
of these who are members of my family, you did it to me."*

*Then he will say to those at his left hand, "You that are
accursed, depart from me into the eternal fire prepared for
the devil and his angels; for I was hungry and you gave me
no food, I was thirsty and you gave me nothing to drink,
I was a stranger and you did not welcome me, naked and
you did not give me clothing, sick and in prison and you
did not visit me." Then they also will answer, "Lord, when
was it that we saw you hungry or thirsty or a stranger or
naked or sick or in prison, and did not take care of you?"
Then he will answer them, "Truly I tell you, just as you did
not do it to one of the least of these, you did not do it to
me." And these will go away into eternal punishment, but
the righteous into eternal life.*[1]

## HELL

There is an awful lot of judgment found in Matthew. Matthew is
one of the few gospels that speaks of a punishment in hell for those
who did not get with Jesus' program. Jesus said very little to sug-
gest there would be an everlasting punishment (or an everlasting

1. Matt 25:31–46.

reward, for that matter) after death. There are only eight references to what we might call "hell" in the gospels. In addition to the story of the rich man and Lazarus in Luke's gospel (where there is not a literal hell, but a shadowy existence in Sheol after death), there are six sets of sayings found in the gospel of Matthew and one saying in Mark's account. [2] In these parables, Matthew declares that people whose lives do not produce the good fruit of compassion and generosity will be "thrown into the furnace of fire" or "cast into the outer darkness" where there will be "weeping and gnashing of teeth." These phrases are unique to Matthew, and many scholars agree that these are ideas and words of Matthew's author alone and not of Jesus. In this particular gospel passage, the reality of an eternal life and an eternal punishment are not characteristic of the historical Jesus.

The English word "hell" with its undying worm and unquenchable fire has been misleadingly substituted in some Bible translations for the Greek word Gehenna (GHEH-en-nah), a term that referred to the Valley of Hinnom—in Hebrew "Ge Hinnom" (gay-hin-NOME)—one of the two principal valleys surrounding the Old City of Jerusalem. Historians believe this valley had been a site where Canaanite followers of prosperity gods like Baal (BAH-al) and Moloch (MOH-lock) sacrificed their first-born children by fire. It is commonly thought that the valley later became the general disposal site for all the refuse of Jerusalem. It has been said that the dead bodies of criminals, the carcasses of animals, and the city's rubbish were burned there in a constantly tended fire. Gehenna thus became a symbol for punishment or destruction after death. The undying worm (or maggots) and unquenchable fire referenced by Mark 9:48 are also stock biblical images for the destruction of evil. The book of Isaiah ends with this verse:

> And they shall go out and look at the dead bodies of the
> people who have rebelled against me; for their worm shall

---

2. Matt 8:12, Matt 13:42, Matt 13:50, Matt 22:13, Matt 24:51, Matt 25:30, and Mark 9:48.

*not die, their fire shall not be quenched, and they shall be an abhorrence to all flesh.*[3]

So, we see a handful of references to punishment after death in the gospels, mostly from one author. The question addressed by biblical scholars is whether these sayings originated with Jesus or whether they served the purpose of the authors we call Matthew and Mark and therefore originated with them. The authenticity of these sayings must finally come down to the question of who Jesus was and what he was about. Jesus preached love for one's enemies, urged continual forgiveness toward those who have hurt us, and told us to pray for those who persecute us. Does this teacher of radical love and compassion then turn around and condemn people to an eternity of suffering in some form of final retribution? Does Jesus believe that a God of love—a compassionate, welcoming, accepting father—will ultimately treat God's children this way? Many conservative Christians would enthusiastically say "Yes!" because the existential fear of eternal punishment is the foundation of their belief system. But I think not.

## THE SON OF MAN

Jesus generally rejected the titles of "messiah" or "son of God" that others thrust on him. According to the gospels, the only title he used for himself was "the son of man" or "the son of adam." No one else calls Jesus by this term. It was an image he apparently claimed for himself, but which the church has generally dropped in favor of "son of God." However, where the phrase "son of man" is used in the gospel accounts, modern English translators often capitalize it as "Son of Man" to ensure that we will understand the use of the term in a very specific context—as a reference to a seemingly supernatural figure found in the apocalyptic book of Daniel in the Hebrew Bible. In Daniel's dream, this figure comes before God on the clouds of heaven and is given dominion over a never-ending

3. Isa 66:24.

empire on earth.[4] The Son of Man fits nicely with the exalted image of Jesus in that other apocalyptic New Testament book—Revelation. But the phrase "son of man" has other connotations in the Hebrew Bible.

For a better understanding of this term, it is helpful to look at Walter Wink's groundbreaking book, *The Human Being: Jesus and the Enigma of the Son of the Man* (2002). Wink explains that in much of the Hebrew Bible the term "son of man" or "*ben 'adam*" (*bane aw-DAWM*) was used to describe humanity in general or a specific human being—conveying the connotation of ordinary human mortality and weakness. (The Hebrew word "*adam*" (*aw-DAWM*) can be translated as either "man" or "Adam" depending on the context.) Similar to the Hebrew idiom "son of wickedness," which refers to a wicked man, the phrase "son of man," or more properly "the son of the man," simply means "a human being." Many scholars insist that when Jesus used the term, he meant he was just one of the boys, a regular fellow. Of course, the phrase comes across as very male-oriented, and it is. Wink suggests that if we prefer, we can translate it as "child of the human" or "'the human one.'" When rendering "*ben 'adam*" in English, translators sometimes use "human being," "mere man," or "O mortal" as substitutions. We see this usage frequently in translations of the book of Ezekiel in the Hebrew Bible, where Yahweh employs the term to refer to the prophet Ezekiel, to whom Yahweh appears in a bizarre vision. There are 107 occurrences of *ben 'adam* in the Hebrew Bible, 93 of which are found in the book of Ezekiel.

## THE CORE OF THE STORY

I am uncomfortable with how Matthew wraps the story around a final judgment that includes an eternal reward and punishment. And I am particularly disturbed by the apocalyptic vision of the Son of Man, angels, and the throne of glory. None of these elements sounds like the historical Jesus to me.

---

4. Dan 7:13–14.

*When the Son of Man comes in his glory, and all the angels with him, then he will sit on the throne of his glory. All the nations will be gathered before him, and he will separate people one from another as a shepherd separates the sheep from the goats, and he will put the sheep at his right hand and the goats at the left.[5]*

Instead, we have to look at the core of the story, which is about the care of the suffering oppressed: the hungry, the thirsty, the naked, the stranger, the sick, and those who are in prison. The voice of Jesus is there. Jesus builds on the foundations of the Hebrew Bible that show Yahweh's care for widows, orphans, and strangers (immigrants).

*God . . . executes justice for the orphan and the widow, and loves the strangers, providing them with food and clothing. You shall also love the stranger, for you were strangers in the land of Egypt.[6]*

I believe that the stories Jesus may have told—like the parable of the rich man and Lazarus, or the last judgment by the Son of Man—were not about our contemporary understanding of life after death in heaven or hell; they were stories about the importance of heaven and hell in this world—paying attention to the beggars at our gates. As the reformer John Calvin (1509–1564) once said, "Hell is not a place but a condition." It is a daily human condition for far too many people. The followers of Jesus are not called to consign unbelievers to a place of suffering after death, but to deliver all people from the living hell of destitution, hunger, illness, and violence.

---

5. Matt 25:31–33.
6. Deut 10:17–19.

# CHAPTER 12

# THE CONSPIRACY OF LOVE

*Now after John was arrested, Jesus came to Galilee,*
*proclaiming the good news of God, and saying,*
*'The time is fulfilled, and the kingdom of God has come near;*
*repent and believe in the good news.*

—THE GOSPEL OF MARK 1:14

*The decisive time has arrived, for the conspiracy of love*
*is rising up to challenge the unjust systems of the world.*
*Change your whole way of thinking and living,*
*and risk everything for this radical message of hope.*

—MY PARAPHRASE OF MARK 1:14

THE KINGDOM OF GOD is the term Jesus used to express his vision of a profound transformation of human beings and human
institutions—social, political, economic and religious—to fully
express the radical character and nature of God—a God of love. To
accomplish this vision, Jesus worked toward the creation of a new

kind of community dedicated to values of compassion, generosity, peace, and justice. He was creating a movement for change, a people engaged in a vast conspiracy of love.

The kingdom of God would have none of the usual hallmarks of an earthly kingdom, nor would it descend from on high with a trumpet blast, accompanied by angels. It was first a kingdom of nobodies, the ragtag rabble of Jesus' followers, the desperately poor and hungry of the world. It drew in people on the bottom of the economic ladder and on the margins of society, people who were rejected by the righteous. They gladly welcomed being part of this new community.

When asked when the kingdom would arrive, Jesus said it was already here. It was already in their midst and spread out all around them, but the wealthy, the well-mannered, and the self-righteous could not see it. It belonged instead to the outcasts of the world: the tax collectors, prostitutes, beggars, shepherds, and other "sinners." It included sick, disabled, and disfigured people who were hungry for wholeness and healing.

Robert Funk (1926–2005), a biblical scholar and founder of the Jesus Seminar, wrote:

> In his parables, Jesus issues an invitation to cross over to God's domain. The rich are unable to find the door to the kingdom, but the poor, the hungry, the sad don't even have to look for it. That is because only those morally and religiously disqualified may enter. Put differently, insiders are out; outsiders are in.[1]

This was the kingdom and the community that Jesus was creating. It was open to anyone who wanted to take part in his vision, but he said they must turn around and develop a new focus. To become an outsider, the rich and righteous must think differently and change the direction of their lives. They must embrace the poor and the sick and accept those they formerly looked down upon as their new family, their new brothers and sisters. The kingdom involves a new way of thinking and seeing. The gospels state

---

1. Funk, *Quest of the Historical Jesus*, 21.

that Jesus called on people to repent and believe in the good news that he was proclaiming.

## REPENT

To our ears, repentance usually conveys a sense of guilt and regret. It is commonly understood as a feeling of remorse, and that is precisely how the church has conventionally used the term. But repent doesn't capture the true meaning of the Greek word *metanoia* (*met-AN-oy-ah*) meaning a fundamental shift or movement (*meta*) of the mind (*noia*). It is a movement that takes us beyond the mindset of our cultural traditionalism—our conventional wisdom—into a new way of perceiving and thinking about the world around us. The repentance that Jesus speaks of is a transformative movement, a fundamental change of life that is deeper, more basic, and more far-reaching than our common understanding of the word repentance. It is not about being sorry for the past. It is about thinking differently and changing the direction of our lives for the future. Metanoia essentially means to turn around, to change the form, to take on a whole new identity. It involves a change of orientation, direction, or character that is so pronounced and dramatic that the very form and purpose of a life is decisively altered and reshaped. It means to begin the journey of walking away from the old to the new.

To Jesus, metanoia was a change so dramatic that it implied starting over again through a metaphorical second birth. He declared, "I tell you the truth, no one can see the kingdom of God without being born again." Jesus was articulating an invitation to a new quality of life in the midst of the old. It is a fundamental transformation that enables us to begin the journey of a new life. It is like being reborn with a radically new perspective on the meaning of life.

The deep-seated change of metanoia that Jesus describes happens through a process of learning and growing. It involves learning a completely new way of thinking about life, being instructed in a new way of seeing reality. It means discarding conventional wisdom and traditional common sense for an unconventional wisdom and a transformed sense of purpose. Start by turning around and going the other way, Jesus says to us. You are a captive of your culture and, although you may not be able to see it, you are headed in the wrong direction. You are living in darkness, mired in confusion.

Being born again is not about religion. It is about a new way of living. It is a movement from greed to giving, from selfishness to servanthood, from social conformity to insurrection against the status quo. Jesus was talking about shifting allegiances and values away from a mainstream culture of power, domination, and violence to the kingdom values of selfless love, compassion, humility, equality, generosity, forgiveness, justice, peace, service, and inclusive community. This is what it means to be born anew. It is a movement from values that focus solely on "me" to the embrace of values focused on "you" and "us" in a life of mutuality and service.

## BELIEVE

The English verb *believe* is a translation of the Greek *pisteuó* (*pist-YOO-oh*) which can mean to believe, but more accurately means to trust or to have faith in. It is based on the noun *pistis* (*PIS-tis*) that means faith, belief, trust, confidence, and faithfulness. Normally, belief has the connotation of an intellectual acceptance of a proposition—a certainty that something is true, even in the absence of empirical evidence. Faith, likewise, implies great confidence in an idea. But faith is often a visible and outward expression of what is believed to be true in one's head. Further, faith is a trust in something to the extent that one would be willing to bet one's life on it. To be faithful within the context of any culture is to be seized by and devoted to whatever is believed to matter most in one's life. Belief is a psychological state, while faith is a way of living.

## A RADICAL MESSAGE OF HOPE

The good news that Jesus proclaimed was a radical message of hope for people at the bottom of his society—the peasants and fisherfolk of Galilee. Jesus called on his followers to trust that the way of life he was teaching and modeling had the capability of transforming their lives and ultimately could change the world. He invited them to transform their old ways of thinking, and to shed their culture's conventional wisdom in order to follow him. He asked them to risk their lives for this new way of living when he said, "If any want to become my followers, let them deny themselves and take up their cross daily and follow me." Taking up one's cross in the context of first-century Roman Palestine meant a willingness to sacrifice one's life in an engagement with political and economic power and a challenge to the unjust systems of the world.

So, both *metanoia* and *pistis* involve a committed change—a revolution in one's way of thinking and perceiving, and a life dedicated to that new reality, trusting that this is the right thing to do, that this is the most important thing to do, and that this new way is worth risking everything one has, including one's life.

As followers of Jesus, we are called to pursue justice on behalf of the vast majority of people all around the world who suffer under pervasive domination systems. The reign of God is about doing for the entire human family what we do within our individual families. Loving the whole human family means ensuring that everyone gets a fair and equitable access to the necessary means of life: food, clean water, clothing, shelter, education, health care, meaningful employment, safety, and protection from violence.

It is up to us to figure out how to live together as a human community, how to love one another, and how to care for the earth and all its creatures. If we live our lives as co-conspirators with Jesus, if we engage in his conspiracy of love in our time and place, his vision of the inbreaking reign of love will be fulfilled within us and through us one small sacred act at a time. And all we need is love.

# BIBLIOGRAPHY

Bonhoeffer, Dietrich. *Letters and Papers from Prison*. New York: Macmillan, 1972

Buttrick, David. *Speaking Parables*. Louisville: Westminster John Knox, 2000.

Donahue, *The Gospel in Parable*. Minneapolis: Fortress, 1988.

Douglas, Frederick. Speech delivered on August 3, 1857, at Canandaigua, New York.

Ellul, Jacques. *The Meaning of the City*. Eugene, OR: Wipf and Stock, 2011.

———. *The Subversion of Christianity*. Grand Rapids: Eerdmans, 1991.

Funk, Robert. "The Quest of the Historical Jesus: Problem and Promise." *Intersections*: Vol. 1998: No. 5, Article 8.

Funk, Robert, Roy Hoover, and the Jesus Seminar. *The Five Gospels: the Search for the Authentic Words of Jesus*. New York: Macmillan, 1993.

Graham, "New Lost Cause." *The Atlantic*, October 18, 2021. https://www.theatlantic.com/ideas/archive/2021/10/donald-trumps-new-lost-cause-centers-january-6/620407/

Herzog, William R. *Parables as Subversive Speech*. Louisville: Westminster / John Knox, 1994.

Jeremias, Joachim. *Jerusalem in the Time of Jesus*. Philadelphia: Fortress Press, 1969.

Jordan, Clarence. *Cotton Patch Parables of Liberation*. Scottsdale, PA: Herald, 1970.

———. *The Cotton Patch Version of Mattew and John*. Chicago: Association, 1970.

Kraybill, Donald. *The Upside-Down Kingdom*. Scottsdale, PA: Herald, 1978.

Living Wage Calculator for Wayne County, MI. February 14, 2024. http://livingwage.mit.edu/places/2616322000

McLaren, Brian. *Everything Must Change*. Nashville: Thomas Nelson, 2007.

Paradis, "Lost Cause's Long Legacy." *The Atlantic*, June 26, 2020. https://www.theatlantic.com/ideas/archive/2020/06/the-lost-causes-long-legacy/613288/

Schade, Leah D. "The Widow's Mite? No, MIGHT—Justice, Power, and the Widow," Progressive Christian blog on *Patheos*, November 11, 2018.

https://www.patheos.com/blogs/ecopreacher/2018/11/widow-mite-widow-might-justice-power-coins/

Schultz, Valerie. "From the Gospels to Elizabeth Warren, women nevertheless persist," *America*, March 29, 2017. https://www.americamagazine.org/faith/2017/03/29/gospels-elizabeth-warren-women-nevertheless-persist/

Scott, Bernard Brandon. *Hear then the Parable: A Commentary on the Parables of Jesus.* Minneapolis: Fortress Press, 1989.

Wink, Walter. *The Powers That Be.* New York: Doubleday, 1998.

www.ingramcontent.com/pod-product-compliance
Lightning Source LLC
Chambersburg PA
CBHW071051090426
42737CB00013B/2324